The
Economist

Pocket Banker

The Economist

Pocket Banker

Tim Hindle

Basil Blackwell, Oxford and New York

and

The Economist

© Tim Hindle, 1985

Jointly published 1985 by
Basil Blackwell, Ltd.
108 Cowley Road, Oxford OX4 1JF
and *The Economist*
25 St. James's Street, London SW1A 1HG

Basil Blackwell, Inc.
432 Park Avenue South, Suite 1505
New York, New York 10016

Library of Congress Cataloging in Publication Data
Hindle, Tim.
The Economist pocket banker.
Includes index.
1. Banks and banking—Dictionaries. I. Title
II. Title: Pocket banker.
HG151.H56   1985   332.1′ 03′ 21   85 – 4047
ISBN 0-631-14003-4

British Library Cataloguing in Publication Data
Hindle, Timothy
The Economist pocket banker,
1. Banks and banking
Title
332.1   HG601

Typeset by Katerprint Co. Ltd, Oxford
Printed in Great Britain by T. J. Press Ltd, Padstow

Contents

Preface

My hope is that this book will instruct and entertain, not necessarily in that order. Banking and finance are subjects with their own dialect, a dialect that makes opaque the layman's view of quite simple subjects. Start by remembering that bankers are little more than sophisticated barrow boys, hawking loans and on the scrounge for other people's money (deposits). Banker-speak is one part of a centuries-old conspiracy to camouflage the basic nature of their business.

But their dialect also sometimes betrays them. They talk a lot of markets. And it is helpful to think of the City of London (or of any other financial centre) as a number of different market places where different financial products are packaged and sold. As anywhere else, the market stall and the corner shop are being-replaced by the supermarket and the boutique. Communicating with a bank should be no more daunting than walking into Safeways or telephoning a mail order company.

The book is a combination of at least three things – a dictionary, an encyclopaedia, and a book of records. It is a bit of each and comprehensively none of them. A lot more space and energy would be required for it to be more. My reasons for the formula are no more advanced than that I believe it makes banking a bit more fun, and may help strip away some of the mystery for laymen and students from a subject that more and more hits the headlines from Manchester to Mexico.

My thanks are due to many people for helping in the production of this book: to Elizabeth Bland, Penny Butler and Christopher Hutton-Williams for tussling with a less than perfect manuscript; to Patrick Frazer for pointing out some unpardonable errors; to my colleagues on *The Economist*, Robert Willis who compiled the statistical tables, Bobby Hunt who drew the cartoons and Kevin Kallaugher who drew the caricatures. Not least of all my thanks are due to my wife, Ellian, who cheerfully coped with a long series of solitary weekends whilst I scribbled my way from A to Z.

Tim Hindle, September 1984

A

A forfait. The business of discounting instruments (like BILLS OF EXCHANGE) that are used to finance the export of CAPITAL GOODS. Banks buy the exporter's bills at a DISCOUNT. The *à forfait* market grew up in Switzerland, where it concentrated on buying East–West trade debts. In recent years its centre has shifted to London and its name has become anglicized to forfaiting (not to be confused with forfeiting).

One of the most successful banks in the business is the Hungarian International Bank, a London subsidiary of Hungary's CENTRAL BANK, and a bank not afraid to motivate its workers. In 1983, its managing director, an Englishman, Mr Jack Wilson, was one of the most highly paid bankers in London. He earned £216,742.

Abs, Hermann. The honorary chairman of DEUTSCHE BANK and the leading figure in West German post-war banking. He once held so many directorships that the West Germans passed a law (lex Abs) limiting the permissible number for any one person.

When aged over 80, Mr Abs was still active. In 1982, he was made a special adviser to the Vatican's bank, the Istituto per l'Opere di Religione, in its discussions with the Italian government over settlements arising from the collapse of BANCO AMBROSIANO. At the end of 1983 he emerged again as the mastermind of the German financing of the purchase, at the London auctioneers Sotheby's, of a twelfth-century German book, the Gospels of Henry the Lion. At £7.4 million it was then the most expensive work of art ever to be sold at auction.

Acceptance. A BILL OF EXCHANGE that has been endorsed by a bank – i.e. the bank has given its GUARANTEE that payment will be forthcoming from it, if not from the buyer: a popular way of financing trade. The exporter who gets his bills accepted by a first-class bank (like a member of the ACCEPTING HOUSES COMMITTEE) can then sell the bills at a DISCOUNT and get immediate payment for the goods he has exported.

Accepting Houses Committee (AHC). An exclusive club of seventeen independent British merchant banks whose original common denominator was their ACCEPTANCE business – putting their name to traders' BILLS to make them LIQUID (sellable). For a while the seventeen had exclusive privileges with the BANK OF ENGLAND. Bills they had accepted would always, if necessary, be bought by the Bank. But those days are disappearing. A long list of banks (over 120) now has the same privileges. However, the AHC is still a powerful force in the CITY of London and still terribly British. When member Antony Gibbs became a wholly-owned subsidiary of the HONGKONG AND SHANGHAI BANKING CORPORATION, it had to leave.

Table 1 *Accepting houses members banks committee*

	Assets (at 31st December 1983)	Acceptances (£m)	Net Profit (£m)
Kleinwort, Benson, Lonsdale	3800	440	22
Schroders	3093	292	9
Hill Samuel[1]	2857	205	25
Samuel Montagu	3242	305	11
Morgan Grenfell	2740	425	16
Hambros[1]	3240	530	10
S. G. Warburg & Co[1]	2017	274	20
N. M. Rothschild	1593	162	2
Lazard Brothers	1235	68	7
Baring Brothers	1077	147	1
Charterhouse Japhet	848	85	8
Guinness Mahon[2]	509	51	2
Singer & Friedlander	478	86	3
Brown Shipley	465	69	3
Robert Fleming	288	13	2
Rea Brothers	190	25	1

Notes:
[1] March 31st, 1984 [2] September 30th, 1983
Source: Company reports

Access. The British CREDIT CARD owned by three big banks LLOYDS, MIDLAND and NATIONAL WESTMINSTER, and one little one, WILLIAMS & GLYN'S. Access did much to discredit credit cards in Britain. It was launched in 1972 by a mail shot that put unsolicited cards into the hands of hundreds of hostile bank customers. Its famous advertising slogan, 'Access takes the waiting out of wanting', grated on the ears of many conservative Englishmen for whom waiting was a highly desirable part of wanting.

Although launched six years after its rival, BARCLAYCARD, Access's annual turnover (the value of all purchases made with the card) now exceeds that of its rival. However, there is little to choose between them, and their tariffs differ almost impercept-ibly. Access is a member of the MASTERCARD and EUROCARD networks.

Table 2 *The two big British credit cards*

	Access	Barclaycard
Launched	1972	1966
Cardholders (end–1983)	6.85m	6.84m
Average monthly new cards issued	66,000	44,000
Value of cardholders' purchases (1983)	£3.153 billion	£2.712 billion
Annual rate of increase of value of purchases	30%	24%

Account. The balance of a customer's borrowing and lending with a bank.

In Britain, an account is also the period of two weeks on the London stockmarket prior to SETTLEMENT DAY. No payment is required until settlement day for SECURITIES bought within an account. This tends to give an artificial boost to the stockmarket in the first few days of a new account: investors hope to buy and sell within the account and make a profit with no outlay. After holidays have been deducted, there are twenty-four accounts in a year.

Actuary. According to one apocryphal definition, someone who finds accounting too exciting. An actuary calculates probabili-ties, usually for insurance companies that need to set their PRE-MIUMS according to how likely it is that the event they are insuring will happen. Actuaries therefore spend much of their time considering the probability that others will die within a certain period.

Administrator. A new type of RECEIVER created by the British government's latest legislation on BANKRUPTCY. A company near to INSOLVENCY, or any of its creditors, will be able to ask a court to appoint an administrator. The administrator will have to come up with a rescue plan for the company and, if its creditors approve the plan, all its debts will be frozen for at least six months while the administrator sets to work trying to keep the company out of CAREY STREET.

African Development Bank. The little sister of the development banks (see INTER-AMERICAN DEVELOPMENT BANK, ASIAN DEVELOP-MENT BANK). Based in Abidjan on the Ivory Coast, the African Development Bank is financed by rich member countries of the ORGANIZATION FOR ECONOMIC CO-OPERATION AND DEVELOPMENT and lends to poor African ones. In 1983 it approved thirty-five loans worth $574 million compared with thirty-three loans worth $399 million in 1982: 33 per cent of its 1983 lending went to public utility projects, 24 per cent to transport and 23 per cent to agriculture: 40 per cent of its loans went to East Africa.

Agent bank. The bank appointed by the lenders in a SYNDICATED LOAN to look after the loan throughout its life. INTEREST and CAPITAL repayments on the loan are channelled through the agent bank for forwarding to all the other participants in the loan. It is the agent bank that has the hassle of chasing up late payers.

AKA. A West German company financed by a pool of fifty-eight COMMERCIAL BANKS in order to give EXPORT CREDITS of more than one year's MATURITY.

Allkonto. An original kind of bank ACCOUNT first designed in Sweden by its biggest bank, Svenska Handelsbanken, in the mid-1970s, versions of which can now be found in many parts of the world. An all-singing, all-dancing type of account that com-bines a money transmission service (CHEQUES, etc.) with an IN-TEREST-bearing savings account and a loan facility.

American Depositary Receipt (ADR). A device to enable Amer-ican investors to buy foreign shares without going abroad. The

ADR is a piece of paper issued by an American bank which gives the purchaser the rights to an underlying share held by the bank at its overseas offices. The advantage of ADRs to the investor lies in their simplicity: they are denominated in dollars, and their DIVIDENDS come in without having to scan foreign publications to find out how to receive them.

The biggest bank in the business of issuing ADRs is MORGAN GUARANTY, which invented them in 1927. There are now more than 550 foreign shares available to American investors in the form of ADRs. In 1978 there were fewer than 400 and in 1961 only 150. The country with the most shares in ADR form is Japan with 132, followed by Australia with 109, Britain with 100 and South Africa with 90. Trailing them come West Germany, Sweden, Italy, Holland, France, Mexico, Norway, Jamaica, Zambia, Israel, Belgium and HONGKONG.

American Express. The Coca-Cola of financial service companies; a conglomerate whose name is a household word around the world. Its most famous products are its TRAVEL AND ENTERTAINMENT CARDS and its TRAVELLER'S CHEQUES. But it also owns a big American insurance company, Fireman's Fund, the WALL STREET BROKERage firms of Shearson and Lehman Brothers, and the Swiss-based Trade Development Bank.

The whole huge business was built up on the money that customers gave the company to buy its traveller's cheques. While the customers sat on their cheques (sometimes for years, but on average for about three months), American Express used their cash to earn itself INTEREST. Just shows what you can do with one bright idea.

Amortization. American for DEPRECIATION.

Annualized percentage rate (APR). A standardized measure of annual RATES of INTEREST defined by Britain's Consumer Credit Act. It was designed to stop loan sharks from misleadingly advertising their rates of interest as, say, 'only 2 per cent' when what they meant was 2 per cent per month. Now they have to publish their rate as an APR (i.e. what it is equivalent to if converted into a single annual interest payment). The APR for 2 per cent per month is 26.82 per cent, calculated by the formula:

$$APR = 100 \left(1 + \frac{rate}{100}\right)^{n} - 100$$

where n is the number of payments per year.

AR 11. The annual return that Britain's BUILDING SOCIETIES have to send to their regulator, the CHIEF REGISTRAR OF FRIENDLY SOCIETIES. It is full of useful information on such things as the ages of the directors and loans that the society has made to organizations in which the directors have an interest. Societies' depositors have a right to receive a copy of the AR 11 if they ask for it. Regrettably, the AR 11 is to disappear under proposed new legislation for the building societies.

Arbitrage. Taking advantage of price differences in two markets to buy in one and sell in the other at a profit. For example, in the foreign exchange markets there are sometimes differences in CROSS-RATES for currencies in different FINANCIAL CENTRES. These can make it possible to buy, say, US dollars for yen in SINGAPORE and sell them in London for sterling and then back into yen in New York – all for a profit.

Asian Development Bank. A LONG-TERM lending institution set up in 1966 to foster economic growth in member countries (developing ones in Asia and the Pacific region). Its headquarters are in Manila.

The bank has forty-five members from inside and outside Asia. They all subscribe to the bank's CAPITAL, 64 per cent of which comes from countries within the region. The money is lent to poorer countries for between ten and thirty years with a two- to seven-year GRACE PERIOD – the sort of lending that is not available from COMMERCIAL BANKS.

The biggest borrowers from the ADB have been Indonesia, the Philippines, South Korea, Pakistan and Thailand. About 30 per cent of its loans go to agricultural projects.

Asset. A thing of value owned by a company or an individual. Banks have three different types of asset.

- Financial assets (the great majority) include their loans, BILLS and opther financial instruments;
- Fixed assets are objects like branches that are difficult to move;
- Intangible assets are things like goodwill and patents.

Asset management. The art of optimizing the return that a bank gets on its ASSETS (i.e. loans, etc.). This involves finding a balance between the YIELD from the assets and their RISK, MATURITY and LIQUIDITY. Before there was any real competition for savers' deposits, banks looked after their assets and let their LIABILITIES take care of themselves. Now there is a new art called LIABILITY MANAGEMENT.

Association of International Bond Dealers (AIBD). A loosely knit club that brings together dealers and UNDERWRITERS of international BONDS. The AIBD aspires to be no more than a standard-setting body, taking on none of the wider responsibilities of REGULATING or acting as a CLEARING HOUSE for its members.

At call. Money at call is money deposited by a bank or with a bank that has no fixed date of maturity. It can be withdrawn at any time when the depositor "calls" for it.

Automated clearing house (ACH). A CLEARING HOUSE that works not with paper things like CHEQUES but with electronic orders to debit and credit different ACCOUNTS at banks that are members of the ACH.

Automated teller machine (ATM). Commonly used to refer to any machine that does things that would have been done by a bank teller fifteen years ago. More strictly, ATMs should be distinguished from CASH dispensers (CDs), which dispense only cash (and which should not be confused with CERTIFICATES OF DEPOSIT). ATMs can do more things, like take orders for CHEQUE books, hand out statements or take in deposits.

In the last ten years ATMs have spread like convolvulus, both inside bank branches and through their walls (see table). They could make 60 per cent of all bank staff redundant. If they don't, HOME BANKING might.

. . . 1965. . . .

. . . . 1975. . . .

. . . . 1985. . . .

. . . . 1995. . . .

Table 3 *Automated teller machines[1]*

Network operator	Country	ATMs	Cards (million)
Carte Bleue	France	2,520	3.70
Crédit Agricole	France	2,101	5.90
Mitsui Trust & Banking	Japan	1,637	2.63
Lloyds Bank	Britain	1,538	2.88
National Westminster Bank	Britain	1,474	2.05
Societa Interbancario Automazione	Italy	1,431	2.15
Magic Line	US	1,400	2.40
Dai-Ichi Kangyo Bank	Japan	1,377	4.38
Bank of America	US	1,326	1.20
Fuji Bank	Japan	1,300	3.62

Notes:
[1] end 1983
Source: Nilson Report

Aval. A sort of continental European ACCEPTANCE – a GUARANTEE on a BILL OF EXCHANGE.

B

Bad debt. What all bankers detest but without which they would not be in business: the loan that goes bad (i.e. is not repaid). Banks know that as surely as the sun rises in the morning they will have bad debts. Hence they set aside PROVISIONS out of their profits so that when the bad debts come they will not be such a blow to their profits nor as shocking to their shareholders.

Bahamas. A string of islands off the south of Florida with some pretty beaches and a lot of banks. Bahamas developed as a place where American banks could book their international loans free of the inconvenience of domestic regulations and taxes. As America's INTERNATIONAL BANKING FACILITIES have enabled this OFFSHORE BANKING to come back home, the growth in Bahamian banking business has slowed down.

Bahnhofstrasse. A street in Zurich traversed by trams. At one end stands the Swiss National Bank, the country's CENTRAL BANK; at the other the main railway station. Between the two sit all the gnomes that matter. Dominating them are the big three Swiss banks – SWISS BANK CORPORATION, CREDIT SUISSE and UNION BANK OF SWITZERLAND.

Bahrain. An island off the east coast of Saudi Arabia to which it will one day be attached by a causeway. Bahrain has become the number one FINANCIAL CENTRE in the Middle East, neatly located in a time zone halfway between HONGKONG/SINGAPORE and London, and conveniently close to the Gulf oil wealth.

Bahrain built up a profitable expertise in dealing in Gulf currencies when the domestic banks of the Gulf countries themselves were too unsophisticated to handle them. Recently, however, countries like Kuwait, the United Arab Emirates and Saudi Arabia have become concerned at the way in which their currencies have become internationalized through Bahrain. They have successfully tried to slow down the flow of their money to the island.

Balance of payments. A country's set of accounts with the rest of the world. The accounts can be divided into two: the current account and the capital account.

The current account consists of:

- Visible trade – the imports and exports of goods.
- INVISIBLE TRADE – trade in services such as banking, insurance and tourism. Traditionally, Britain has had a large surplus on its invisible trade which has gone some way (and sometimes all the way) to redressing its deficit on visible trade.
- Transfer payments – things like the REMITTANCES of migrant workers to their homeland and the payment of DIVIDENDS and INTEREST to foreign companies, governments and international organizations.

The capital account consists of LONG-TERM investment – either direct foreign investment (e.g. a company in one country buying a company in another), or PORTFOLIO investment (e.g. a German buying shares on WALL STREET) – and SHORT-TERM capital flows of 'hot money'.

Balloon. A loan whose repayments are not spread evenly over the life of the loan. At one stage (usually towards the end of the loan's life) the dribble of repayments bulges into one or two big final 'balloon' repayments.

Banco Ambrosiano. Once the biggest privately-owned bank in Italy, Banco Ambrosiano collapsed in 1982 under the weight of some peculiar overseas lending orchestrated by its chairman ROBERTO CALVI, who died the same year in London. Out of the ashes of Banco Ambrosiano has arisen a new smaller bank, Nuovo Banco Ambrosiano.

Bank Bumiputra. Malaysia's biggest bank. Set up as a purely Malay bank to counter the dominant Chinese influence in the country's banking system, it got into serious difficulties in the 1980s from, ironically, lending huge sums to Chinese property developers in HONGKONG.

Bank for International Settlements (BIS). A CENTRAL BANK for central bankers housed in a round tower near Basel railway station in Switzerland. Set up in 1930, it is a company owned by central banks, a commercial bank (CITIBANK) and some private individuals. It has become a club for European central bankers (and invited guests) to swap notes and RESERVES. In the 1970s it developed powerful research and statistics departments that became the authority on the burgeoning EUROMARKET.

When the Euromarket developed into an international debt crisis in the early 1980s, the BIS took a forceful role in supplying SHORT-TERM BRIDGING LOANS to dollar-less developing countries until they could get their economies into the shape required for INTERNATIONAL MONETARY FUND LONG-TERM loans. See Table 4 page 21.

BIS's president (until the end of 1984) is FRITZ LEUTWILER, chairman of the SWISS NATIONAL BANK.

Bank of America. For many years the biggest bank in the world. Recently toppled from its pedestal by CITIBANK. Founded by A. P. GIANNINI, the bank, based in California, was scornfully regarded by its cosmopolitan New York rivals as just a provincial hick. Now it is as international as they are with quite as many dud loans to Latin American countries as they have.

Bank of America was the first big bank to think about its wider role in society. In the 1970s, under its erstwhile chairman Mr Tom Clausen, now head of the WORLD BANK, it was in the forefront of a move to develop a form of social accounting for banks.

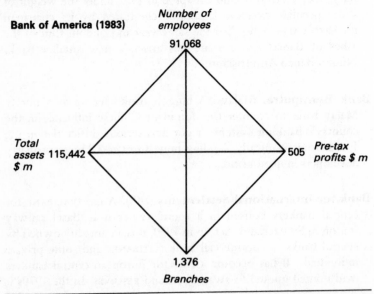

Bank of England. Britain's CENTRAL BANK. Founded in 1694, it is the world's second oldest central bank, being six years younger than Sweden's RIKSBANK. Known affectionately as the OLD LADY OF THREADNEEDLE STREET (the London street on which it has carried out its business for 250 years), it was privately owned until it was nationalized in 1946.

The Bank of England is both monetary authority and bank supervisor, roles that are sometimes separated in other countries. On top of that, it has given itself a general remit to keep an eye on all financial activity in the CITY of London. In 1982, for example, it was involved in cleaning up the LLOYD'S insurance market.

Its special style of supervision – by gentle coercion rather than by rough edict – is much admired around the world and has been given the credit for the safe and successful growth (so far) of the EUROMARKET and of London as the world's number one international banking centre.

Bank of Scotland. Although it sounds like the CENTRAL BANK of Scotland, it is not. The Bank of Scotland is the country's second

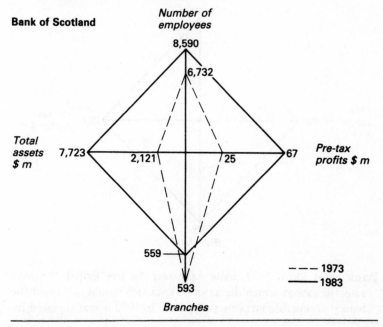

Bank of Scotland

- Number of employees
- 8,590
- 6,732
- Total assets $ m — 7,723 — 2,121 — 25 — 67 — Pre-tax profits $ m
- 559
- 593
- Branches

- – – – 1973
- ——— 1983

biggest COMMERCIAL BANK, 35 per cent owned by England's BARCLAYS BANK. Strong in oil finance from experience with Britain's North Sea, it has offices in HONGKONG and New York, Houston and Moscow.

The Bank of Scotland, founded in 1695, is like a central bank in one respect: it prints its own bank NOTES (as do the other Scottish clearing banks). However, for each note it prints it has to hold one of those printed by the BANK OF ENGLAND.

The governor of the bank (called a chairman in most other banks) is the appropriately named Mr Risk.

Bank of Tokyo. COMMERCIAL BANKS in Japan are more or less indistinguishable, except for the Bank of Tokyo. It has certain privileges under Japan's banking laws which have enabled it to specialize in foreign exchange and trade financing. It is the only Japanese bank whose non-yen ASSETS exceed its yen ones. It is no surprise, then, that the Bank of Tokyo has more overseas offices than any other Japanese bank and very few domestic branches.

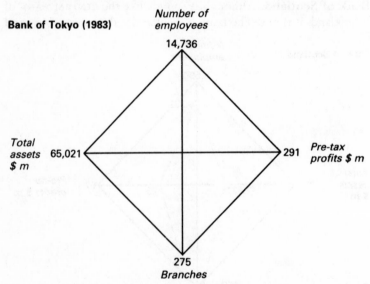

Bank of Tokyo (1983)

Number of employees 14,736

Total assets $ m 65,021

291 *Pre-tax profits $ m*

275 *Branches*

Bank rate. Until 1972, bank RATE was the key British INTEREST rate: the rate at which the BANK OF ENGLAND would DISCOUNT the banks' acceptable BILLS OF EXCHANGE. In 1972 it was replaced by

MINIMUM LENDING RATE. Minimum lending rate was laid to rest in 1981.

Bank Wire. An automated information and money transfer system in the United States owned and run by more than 250 private banks in seventy-five cities. It competes with FEDWIRE.

Bankers' Automated Clearing Services (BACS). The company set up by British banks in 1968 (as Inter-Bank Computer Bureau) to handle electronic payments between them. It is situated in the leafy London suburb of Harrow and has become the biggest automated CLEARING HOUSE in the world, handling 600 million transactions every year – about 20 per cent of all Britain's non-CASH transactions.

The service is now directly available to the banks' customers. Companies, like banks, can deliver their payment instructions to the clearing house on magnetic tape. One estimate suggests that the cost of making a payment through BACS is about one-third the cost of processing old-fashioned paper-based payment systems like CHEQUES.

Banker's draft. An order from a buyer/importer to his bank to make a payment to the bank of the seller/exporter whose goods he has ordered. The draft is sent to the exporter who presents it to his bank for payment. The bank in return presents it to the buyer's bank for reimbursement.

Banking Act, 1979. Britain's first attempt to codify some of the mish-mash of informal regulations that governed the country's mushrooming number of banks. The Act set up two types of institution: RECOGNIZED BANKS and LICENSED DEPOSIT-TAKING INSTITUTIONS. Each type has to have the approval of the BANK OF ENGLAND before opening up shop. To win approval as a recognized bank depends on things like offering a wide range of banking services and being of 'high reputation and standing in the financial community'. Licensed deposit-takers (which offer a narrower range of services and whose directors must all be 'fit and proper persons') sometimes wail that the Act brands them as second-class institutions. The Bank of England insists that this is not so. There are about 290 recognized banks and 310 licensed deposit-takers.

The Act also prescribes the circumstances in which institutions can call themselves banks, and set up Britain's first DEPOSIT PROTECTION FUND for banks.

Banking Insurance and Finance Union (BIFU). Britain's main banking union. In 1979 it changed its name from the National Union of Bank Employees to signal its intention to expand its membership beyond the banking industry. It now has around 152,000 members, compared with 126,000 just before the name change. It has captured some members in the insurance industry and is now making a play for the BUILDING SOCIETIES.

Bankruptcy. The unpleasant condition of being bankrupt, which can be brought upon a debtor by a legal petition either from himself or from an unpaid creditor.

Banque de France. France's CENTRAL BANK. The Banque de France plays a much less significant role than do central banks in other countries of a comparable size. It does not have responsibility for the supervision of the French banking system, nor does it have much control over the operation of monetary policy, which is kept firmly in the hands of the French Treasury.

Banque Nationale de Paris (BNP). France's largest COMMERCIAL BANK (if you exclude CREDIT AGRICOLE from the definition of a commercial bank). BNP, formed in 1966 by the merger of two banks that had been nationalized since 1945, is the most international of the big French banks. It is the most active in the EUROMARKET and has offices in over sixty countries, many of them former French colonies. Inside France BNP has 2,000 branches.

Barclaycard. Britain's oldest bank CREDIT CARD, Barclaycard is also a CHEQUE GUARANTEE CARD. Started in 1966 by Barclays Bank, it began slowly, making losses for the bank for a number of years. It picked up in the late 1970s when plastic banking came of age, and it is still growing very fast. In 1983, its turnover (the value of goods bought with Barclaycards) was up by 24 per cent, and the number of transactions carried out with the cards was up by 20 per cent.

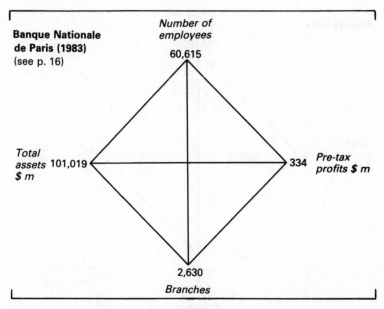

Banque Nationale de Paris (1983) (see p. 16)

Number of employees 60,615

Total assets $ m 101,019

Pre-tax profits $ m 334

2,630 Branches

Barclaycard is one of the biggest members of the international payments network VISA. It continues to experiment with new plastic ways of paying for things. One of its latest experiments is with the oil company Amoco. This allows a petrol purchaser to put his or her Barclaycard into an Amoco pump, press in a PERSONAL IDENTIFICATION NUMBER, take the petrol, retrieve the card and walk away: no paper, no signature, just painful STATE-MENTS (as usual) at the end of the month. See Table 2 on page 3.

Barclays Bank. Britain's biggest bank (but not the biggest bank in Britain; that honour is reserved for NATIONAL WESTMINSTER). Barclays has a lot of business overseas (5,100 branches and offices in eighty-four countries), particularly in the United States and South Africa, which makes its annual general meetings a focus for anti-apartheid groups.

Barclays grew up as an amalgamation of hundreds of small family-owned banks around Britain. Many of the scions of those families can still be found in the higher echelons of the bank today with names like Bevan, Tuke, Tritton, Buxton and, in-deed, Barclay. James Barclay first started a banking business in Lombard Street in 1736.

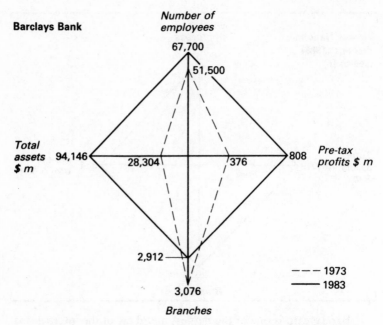

Barclays Bank

Number of employees
67,700
51,500

Total assets $ m 94,146 — 28,304 — 376 — 808 Pre-tax profits $ m

2,912
3,076
Branches

- - - - 1973
——— 1983

Among the British banks Barclays has moved farthest towards becoming a wider financial conglomerate. In 1984 it bought stakes in the STOCKBROKER de Zoete & Bevan (of the same Bevan family) and in the stock JOBBER Wedd Durlacher.

Baring Brothers. The oldest British MERCHANT BANK, founded by Swedish wool merchants who settled in England in the early eighteenth century. Now of moderate size, in the 1890s it was big enough to threaten to bring down the whole of the British banking system after it became overstretched in Argentina – thereby proving that there is nothing new about a Latin American debt crisis. Baring was bailed out by its fellow CITY bankers, but not before the City of London got a shock that it has scarcely forgotten today.

Barter. Paying for goods with other goods – sometimes known as countertrade. At least as old as the Asian silk routes, barter has been enjoying a renaissance in countries hard-pushed to find enough foreign exchange to pay for their imports – i.e. developing countries and Eastern Europe.

Some estimate that barter now accounts for more than 30 per cent of world trade (a trade worth around $590 billion in 1983). One curious recent example was the exchange of American McDonnell Douglas aircraft for Yugoslav hams.

Barter is not very popular with banks, since it threatens to cut out their intermediary role in financing trade. In 1982, the United States introduced legislation allowing banks to set up trading company subsidiaries. Some of them are using the Act to set up companies to engage specifically in barter transactions.

Base rate. The key lending RATE of banks in Britain which acts as a yardstick for other lending and deposit rates. More than 60 per cent of CLEARING BANKS lending is linked to base rate. When newspapers herald an increase in banks' rates, it is base rate they are referring to. Top-quality companies can usually borrow SHORT-TERM at one percentage point above base rate; top-quality individuals often have to pay a lot more.

Bearer bond. A BOND which belongs to whoever bears (i.e. carries) it. All EUROBONDS are issued in bearer form. This adds considerably to their attraction, since it makes their beneficial owner difficult to trace by the likes of tax inspectors. Registered bonds, favoured by domestic bond markets, have their beneficial owners registered with the issuer.

Bed and breakfast. Not eggs and bacon in a boarding house but a way of avoiding enough tax to have champagne in a five-star hotel. The expression refers to the selling of shares at the end of one trading day and the buying back of the same shares the next morning.

There are two good reasons for doing this: either to establish a capital loss to offset against other gains for capital gains tax (CGT) purposes, or to establish a capital gain in order to use up annual exemptions from CGT (in Britain, at present, £5,300 per year).

Biggins, John. An official of the Flatbush National Bank of New York whom history credits with the invention of the bank CRE-DIT CARD in 1946.

Bill (of exchange). A written instruction to a buyer (importer) to pay a seller (exporter) a certain amount of money on a certain date. In Britain a CHEQUE is a type of bill of exchange governed by the Bills of Exchange Act of 1882. (See DRAFT.)

Bill of lading. The document giving title to goods in transit. On the bill is a brief description of the goods and where they are to be delivered. It is signed by the shipper who undertakes to deliver the goods in the same condition as he received them.

Block trading. Trading in big blocks of shares. On the New York Stock Exchange any deal of more than 10,000 shares is a block trade. Such big deals are almost always carried out by institutions such as pension funds or life insurance companies. Some STOCK-BROKERS, like SALOMON BROTHERS, specialize in block trading. The alternative – selling the shares in dribbles – may depress the price undesirably.

Bond. A piece of paper issued by a company or a government promising to repay borrowed money at a prescribed rate of interest to the holder of the piece of paper. Bonds may be bought and sold many times before they are finally redeemed. They come in two forms – registered and bearer. Bearer bonds belong to whoever holds them; registered bonds belong to whoever is registered with the borrower as being their owner.

Bourse. See STOCK EXCHANGE.

Bridging loan. A loan to span from here to there, i.e. a SHORT-TERM, temporary bank loan to tide a borrower over until money promised from elsewhere (e.g. a mortgage loan from a BUILDING SOCIETY or, in the case of a country, a loan from the INTERNATIONAL MONETARY FUND) is forthcoming

Table 4 *BIS bridging loans*

Borrower	Date	Amount ($m)
Argentina	January, 1983	500
Brazil	December, 1982	1,200
	January, 1983	250
Hungary	April, 1982	510
	April, 1983	100
Mexico	August, 1982	1,850
Yugoslavia	March, 1983	300
	June–Sept, 1983	200

Source: BIS

Broker. An umbrella word for anyone who is an agent or go-between in buying or selling financial services or commodities – thus, a stockbroker, an insurance broker or a tea broker.

Budget account. A bank ACCOUNT designed to help individuals to budget for big, bothersome bills. Regular payments into the account of £x per month allow the account holder to make payments of up to £12x during the year, even though that might leave him or her overdrawn for long periods of time.

Building societies. Britain's old but friendly high-street MORT-GAGE shops. Not banks – they are exempted from the BANKING ACT – they take in SHORT-TERM savings and put them out as LONG-TERM loans for buying houses (mortgages). For years, the big British banks had an unwritten agreement not to step on the societies' patch. That was torn up at the end of the 1970s, and in the early 1980s, banks were on occasion providing up to 40 per cent of all mortgage loans.

 Competition from banks has made the societies respond by becoming more like banks. Some now offer CHEQUE books (the

Table 5 *Biggest building societies*

1983:	home town	total assets £m 1983[1]	1963:	total assets £m 1963
Halifax[2]	Halifax	16,782	Halifax	713
Abbey National	London	14,313	Abbey National	485
Nationwide	London	7,348	Co-operative	
Leeds Permanent[3]	Leeds	4,832	Permanent[5]	280
Woolwich			Woolwich	
Equitable[3]	London	4,542	Equitable	222
National &			Leeds Permanent	160
Provincial	Bradford	3,918	Provincial[6]	108
Anglia[4]	Northampton	3,202	Alliance	96
Alliance	Brighton	2,791	Leicester	87
Bradford &	Bingley	2,687	Burnley[6]	77
Bingley				
Leicester	Leicester	2,477	Leek & Moorlands[7]	75

Notes: [1] December 31st [2] January 31st 1984 [3] September 30th 1984 [4] April 4th 1984
[5] Now Nationwide |[6] Merged as National & Provincial [7] Now Britannia
Sources: Building Societies Association, Halifax Building Society

Abbey National), AUTOMATED TELLER MACHINES through the walls of their branches (the Halifax and the Leicester) and HOME BANKING (the Nottingham – in June 1983, one of the first financial institutions in the world to offer its customers banking from home).

So that building societies can become even more like banks two things are changing:

• Tax. Depositors with societies are paid INTEREST NET of basic-rate tax. The societies then pay over to the Inland Revenue tax calculated at the COMPOSITE RATE – a rate designed to take account of the fact that some depositors are non-taxpayers. The 1984 Finance Act equalizes the treatment of banks by bringing their depositors under this same 'composite rate' system.

• Regulation. The societies are governed by philanthropic legislation dating back to 1871, the year Stanley found Livingstone in Africa. New legislation allowing them to increase their limited range of business should be in force in 1986.

Building societies

Year	Number of Societies	Number of Share Accounts 000's	Number of Borrowers 000's	Amount Advanced £m	Total Assets £m
1900	2,286	585			60
1910	1,723	626		9	76
1920	1,271	748		25	87
1930	1,026	1,449	720	89	371
1940	952	2,088	1,503	21	756
1950	819	2,256	1,508	270	1,256
1960	726	3,910	2,349	560	3,166
1970	481	10,265	3,655	1,954	10,819
1976	364	19,991	4,609	6,183	28,202
1977	339	22,536	4,836	6,745	34,288
1978	316	24,999	5,108	8,808	39,538
1979	287	27,878	5,251	9,002	45,789
1980	273	30,636	5,383	9,503	53,793
1981	253	33,388	5,490	12,005	61,815
1982	227	36,607	5,645	15,036	73,033

Bulldog bond. A BOND denominated in sterling but issued by a non-British borrower. In the first four years of the 1980s, thirty-three different non-British states and public- and private-sector companies raised a total of £1.96 billion in bulldog bonds.

Bullet. A loan on which all the PRINCIPAL is repaid in one go at the end of the period of the loan (i.e. for the life of the loan, the borrower is paying only INTEREST).

Bundesbank. West Germany's CENTRAL BANK, housed (rather curiously) in a modern block in a Frankfurt suburb. The Bundesbank's main preoccupation is with controlling inflation inside West Germany. The hyper-inflation of the 1920s is engraved on the Bundesbank's constitution and on the memories of its older directors. The president of the Bundesbank is Karl-Otto Poehl, once a humble journalist.

George Bush. Vice-President of the United States and chairman of a task force drawn up to look at ways in which America's complicated system of bank REGULATION could be simplified. It came out with its recommendations early in 1984. They can only be summarized by a chart.

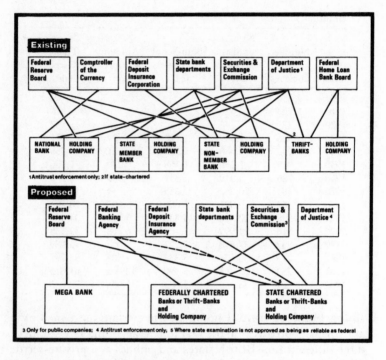

Business expansion scheme. A scheme whereby the British government gives individuals extremely generous tax breaks for investing in small, expanding businesses.

Buyer credit. A MEDIUM- to LONG-TERM loan to the foreign buyer of exported goods. The loan is given by the exporter's bank and usually carries the GUARANTEE of the exporter's national EXPORT CREDIT agency (in Britain's case the EXPORT CREDITS GUARANTEE DEPARTMENT).

The CONSENSUS agreement decrees that buyer credits should not exceed 85 per cent of the price of the goods being bought – i.e. the buyer has to find at least 15 per cent of the purchase price himself, rather like the down payment required on a HIRE PURCHASE agreement.

C

Call money. Money lent by banks to other financial institutions for a rate of INTEREST and on the understanding that it is repayable 'AT CALL' – i.e. on demand.

Call option. The purchased right to buy a currency or a SECURITY at a stated price (the STRIKE PRICE) within a fixed period of time. Hence a call option will be exercised if the SPOT PRICE goes above the strike price. If it is not exercised, the option expires at the end of the fixed period of time and that's that – the cost of the option goes up in smoke.

Calvi, Roberto. The notorious erstwhile chairman of Italy's biggest private bank, BANCO AMBROSIANO, found hanging from scaffolding on London's Blackfriars Bridge one summer morning in 1982. Soon after that Banco Ambrosiano was declared BANKRUPT (with unpaid foreign debts of some $450 million).

Roberto Calvi, an unremarkable man, had some remarkable connections. These stretched from the Vatican and its in-house bank, the Istituto per le Opere di Religione, to the very non-Catholic but powerful Freemasons. His death was assumed (but never proved) to be murder.

CAMEL. The check list of all bank supervisors – the five things they look for when examining a bank:

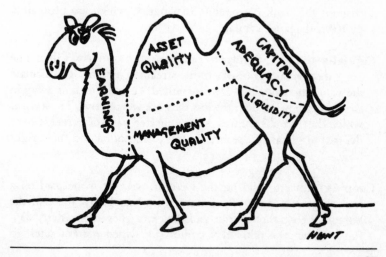

- CAPITAL adequacy.
- ASSET quality.
- Management quality.
- Earnings.
- LIQUIDITY.

Capital. The money used to run a business; a vague term that is made precise only by the addition of a qualifying adjective, e.g. WORKING CAPITAL, paid-up capital (paid up by the shareholders), authorized capital (authorized by the company's memorandum as the amount it can raise) and the most important for banks – free capital (their paid-up capital, RESERVES and BONDS less the amount tied up in FIXED ASSETS, equipment and investments.)

Capital market. A market in long-term financial instruments like bonds or shares. In continental Europe, COMMERCIAL BANKS play a big role in the capital markets both as issuers of instruments and as dealers in second-hand instruments. In America and Britain, the role of commercial banks in the capital markets is more limited. There, INVESTMENT BANKS and MERCHANT BANKS are the main players in the capital markets.

Capital ratio. In most countries, banks' total ASSETS may not exceed some multiple of their CAPITAL and RESERVES. The higher the ratio of capital and reserves to total assets, the more of a cushion the bank has against BAD DEBTS, which are ultimately written off against capital.

Capitalized value. Similar to DISCOUNTED CASH FLOW value. The present (CAPITAL) value of a future stream of income. To calculate the value the payments are discounted – i.e. the further away in the future they are due, the less they are worth now. The RATE at which they are discounted is the expected RATE of INTEREST over the period – that is, the income lost from not having them right now.

Capping. Putting a lid on the RATE of INTEREST to be paid on a FLOATING-RATE loan. When market rates are below the cap, the borrower pays the cap rate and the extra goes into a 'rainy day' fund. When the rainy day comes (i.e. when market rates go above the cap rate), then the fund is used to top up the cap rate being paid by the borrower. Banks cross their fingers that by the time the loan MATURES there is still something left in the fund.

Most banks will not contemplate allowing borrowers to cap their rates unless there are exceptional circumstances (e.g. when the alternative is for them to go bust). Latin America's debt problem is now an exceptional circumstance, and there is some talk of trying to work out a system for capping the interest owed by hard-pressed Latin American countries.

Carat. A measure of the purity of gold: 24 carat gold has nothing mixed with it; 12 carat gold is half gold, half alloy; anything less is scarcely worth hoarding. Pure gold is quite soft, so anyone who wants jewellery to keep its shape should settle for less than the purest.

Carey Street. The street in central London whose name is synonymous with BANKRUPTCY. In it once resided all law firms specializing in putting companies to rest.

Carte à mémoire. A clever little French invention: a plastic card with a built-in microchip that gives it a 'memory'. Information about a cardholder's credit can be fed into the chip and, when purchases are made, the store of credit reduced electronically. When all the credit has been used, the cardholder goes back to his bank to get the card 'topped up' again.

The *carte à mémoire*'s great advantage lies in its ability to be used without constant reference back to the cardholder's bank to find out if he is good for the value of the purchase. Its disadvantage is that the information it contains can too easily be distorted by bending the card.

Cartel. An agreement among the producers of goods or services to FIX the prices of their products. Cartels are not unknown among banks and other financial institutions, but they are notoriously hard to detect. Price behaviour under a cartel can look very like price behaviour under conditions of perfect competition. When big banks' INTEREST RATES move together, do they do so because the banks have agreed on this, or because no one bank can afford to be out of line with the rest?

Cash. Commonly, COIN in the pocket and NOTES in the wallet. For financial institutions, cash can include a wide range of liquid ASSETS – those that can quickly and easily be turned into ready money. In Britain in 1981, 88 per cent of all payments of more than £1 were made with cash. In spite of new technology, cash is still king.

The public's demand for cash varies through the year, being particularly strong over Christmas and other public holidays.

Cash flow. The amount of money flowing through a company in a given period. Variously defined. According to one (fuller) definition, cash flow is a company's new borrowing, plus money from share issues, plus its cash flow from operations (i.e. trading profits and DEPRECIATION minus the increase in working CAPITAL). These cash inflows are equal to cash outflows on capital expenditure, tax and DIVIDENDS, plus what is left to go into RESERVES. A company can be recording increasing profits year by year while its cash flow is taking it to CAREY STREET – for example, Laker Airways (see table). All of its cash went on 'additional investment' (i.e. aircraft) leaving nothing to repay its ever-increasing debts.

Table 6 *Laker Airways' cash flow*

(£m)	1976	1977	1978	1979	1980
Total reported profits	0.9	0.8	1.5	4.8	8.1
Cash inflow					
Operating cash flow	4.5	4.5	12.1	10.7	17.6
Additional borrowing	—	—	11.2	27.3	52.0
Decrease in cash assets	—	2.4	—	2.0	0.8
Total cash flow	4.5	6.9	23.3	40.0	70.4
Cash outflow					
Additional investment	0.5	3.5	19.1	40.0	70.4
Repayment of borrowing	2.1	3.4	—	—	—
Increase in cash assets	1.9	—	4.2	—	—

Note: Little or nothing was paid by Laker in tax. No dividends were paid and no money was raised by share issues.
Source: Professor Tom Lee.

Cash management account. An invention of MERRILL LYNCH, launched in 1977 when America's Treasury Secretary, Donald Regan, was Merrill's boss. The cash management account (CMA) ripped apart America's legislation dividing INVESTMENT BANKING/broking from COMMERCIAL BANKING. In effect, the CMA is a brokerage account that invests savings in a MONEY MARKET FUND. It also gives customers a CHEQUE book, a loan facility and a VISA card (i.e. commercial bank products).

In commercial terms the account has been a runaway success. By the end of 1983 Merrill had opened more than 1 million CMA accounts with savings of over $70 billion. But for years the account was run as a loss leader. Nevertheless, any retail brokerage firm worth its salt now offers a similar product.

Cayman Islands. A Caribbean strand known for its turtles. Like the BAHAMAS, it took advantage of the US restrictions on banks' international business to build itself up as an OFFSHORE BANKING centre. Very little real banking business gets done on the islands. They are essentially a 'booking' centre where deposits and loans get booked rather than actively solicited.

Cedel. (Centrale de Livraison de Valeurs Mobilières). A LUXEMBOURG-based, computerized CLEARING HOUSE for EUROBONDS and other international SECURITIES. CEDEL was founded in 1970 and is now owned by ninety-eight different financial institutions from sixteen countries.

Central bank. The institution at the hub of a country's monetary system. Every developed country (except HONGKONG) has at least one (see BANK OF ENGLAND, BUNDESBANK, FEDERAL RESERVE BOARD, etc.), but not all of them do the same thing. They do, however, all carry out some combination of four different functions: to act as banker to the government, to act as banker to the COMMERCIAL BANKS, to supervise the banking system, and to print and issue the nation's money.

Central market. An expression used to refer to the centralization of trading in SECURITIES, commodities or FUTURES on the floor of one exchange. As computer technology makes dealing away from the floor very much easier and safer, the maintenance of a central market (designed to protect investors from rip-off prices that bear no resemblance to prices in the real marketplace) becomes more difficult.

Certificate of deposit. For large deposits that are not withdrawable on demand, banks issue certificates as evidence of the ownership of the deposit. The certificate is a NEGOTIABLE INSTRUMENT that can be bought and sold in the SECONDARY MARKET. CDs (as they are known) have become an increasingly important source of funds to banks. Since they pay full market RATES, they have pushed up the cost of banks' funds.

Chapter 11. A piece of American legislation that provides troubled companies with protection from baying creditors while the company tries to sort out its problems. A bit like RECEIVERship in Britain and VERGLEICH in West Germany.

In 1978 the rules were changed to allow companies to apply for protection under Chapter 11 before they became unable to repay their bills. Some notorious cases since have led to accusations that the rules are being abused. The asbestos maker Manville Corporation sought the shelter of Chapter 11 because (it said) its LIABILITY under law suits from the victims of asbestos-induced diseases could bankrupt it. Other companies like Continental Airlines have been accused of using Chapter 11 as a means by which to rewrite their labour contracts – a manoeuvre that received the sanction of the Supreme Court early in 1984.

Charterhouse J. Rothschild. One of the most interesting of a new breed of financial conglomerates emerging in the CITY of London. The brainchild of Jacob Rothschild, who split from his family's bank, N. M. ROTHSCHILD, in 1980. He started with an investment trust, RIT & Northern; added 29.9 per cent of London stockbroker Kitcat & Aitken; almost all of L. F. Rothschild Unterberg (no family connection), a New York investment bank; the British merchant bank Charterhouse Japhet; and 24.9 per cent (for £126 million) of the insurance/UNIT TRUST (and pushing into RETAIL BANKING) group, Hambro Life. The group's ambitions to merge fully with Hambro Life was put on a back burner in mid-1984 by stockmarket investors who were not too keen on what they saw as a too-fast-moving hotch-potch.

Chase Manhattan. A big New York bank, once the biggest in the world, now fallen to being (merely) the third biggest in the USA. At one time synonymous in foreigners' eyes with the name of its biggest shareholder David Rockefeller (and therefore with the apogee of American capitalism), it was the first American bank to open an office in Moscow and was later (and famously) chief banker to the Shah of Iran.

More recent blows were the collapse of PENN SQUARE BANK and of the government SECURITIES dealer DRYSDALE GOVERNMENT SECURITIES in 1982. Before it collapsed, Drysdale had grown like Topsy, thanks, in part, to Chase Manhattan's loans. The bank lost about $232 million from Penn Square's and Drysdale's downfall.

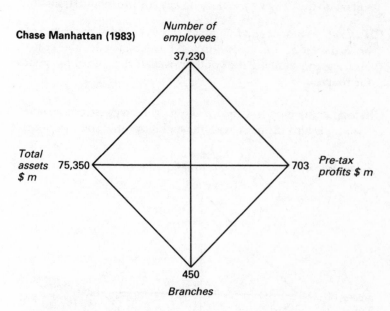

Chase Manhattan (1983)

Number of employees
37,230

Total assets $ m   75,350 — 703   Pre-tax profits $ m

450
Branches

Cheque. A BILL OF EXCHANGE that is drawn on a bank and that is payable on demand. Ever since electronic technology and automated payments came to banking, the demise of the cheque has been predicted. Yet it continues to thrive. It still accounts for the vast majority of non-CASH payments in Britain and the United States. The numbers of cheques passing through the CLEARING SYSTEMS of the two countries continue to increase every year.

Cheque guarantee card. A plastic card used in conjunction with a CHEQUE book. It guarantees the recipient of the cheque that the bank on which the cheque is drawn will meet payments (up to a certain amount) regardless of whether or not the writer of the cheque has that amount of money in his or her ACCOUNT. The introduction of cheque guarantee cards has made cheques almost useless for shopping without a card.

Chief Registrar of Friendly Societies. The supervisor of Britain's BUILDING SOCIETIES. The present incumbent is Michael Bridgeman, a civil servant answerable to the Treasury. As building societies become more like banks, so the Chief Registrar's job becomes more complicated. Increasingly, he consults with the BANK OF ENGLAND on key regulatory questions.

CIF. Cost, insurance and freight: an acronym added to the end of a price quotation to indicate that the price includes the cost of insuring and shipping the goods as well as the cost of the goods themselves.

Citicorp. Not only is Citicorp the world's biggest COMMERCIAL BANK, it is also the bank with the highest profile and the loudest

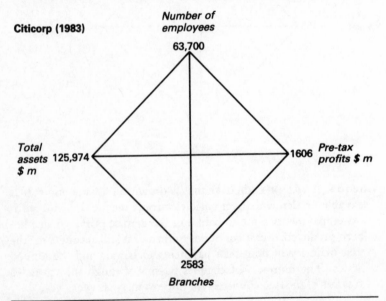

Citicorp (1983)

Number of employees 63,700

Total assets 125,974 $ m

1606 Pre-tax profits $ m

2583 Branches

voice. A sort of King Wenceslas of the banking world in whose footsteps others follow. In the 1960s it was one of the first American banks to become international, hiring a bunch of people from the INTERNATIONAL MONETARY FUND and the WORLD BANK to advise it on lending to the third world – something western banks then knew precious little about.

Nowadays Citicorp has offices in ninety-five countries, more loans abroad than at home and 20 per cent of its profits in Brazil. It has about 60,000 shareholders and the same number of staff.

Citicorp can trace its origins to the City Bank of New York founded in 1812. Confined since 1927 to operating in New York state only, Citicorp has been more aggressive than most in pushing into other states whenever legal loopholes have made that possible. It now has operations in more than forty states.

City. A collective name for the financial institutions in the square mile to the east of St Paul's Cathedral, London. The term is also used to describe the people who work there, as in 'City type', 'City gent', etc.

Table 7 *City of London: overseas earnings*

		1982 (£m)
Banking		1,656
Insurance	Companies	366
	Lloyd's	475
	Brokers	362
Pension funds		287
Baltic Exchange		254
Merchanting		234
Commodities		215
Other brokerage		146
Investment trusts		116
Solicitors		75
Leasing		70
Unit trusts		61
Stock Exchange		44
Lloyds register of shipping		37
	Total	4,369

Source: British Invisible Exports Council

City banks. The twelve Japanese COMMERCIAL BANKS that dominate the country's FINANCIAL SYSTEM (see DIA-ICHI KANGYO). The BANK OF TOKYO, though not officially a City bank, is added to the group for statistical purposes. Not to be confused with CITIBANK, or with a bank in the CITY.

Table 8 *Japan's City banks[1]*

	Net profit (Y b)	% change (on previous year)
Sumitomo	78.4	+31
Fuji	73.0	+29
Mitsubishi	60.1	+48
Dai-Ichi Kangyo	56.4	+52
Sanwa	55.9	+53
Tokai	36.7	+59
Mitsui	33.0	+33
Bank of Tokyo	27.1	+12
Taiyo–Kobe	20.6	+13
Daiwa	15.7	+2
Saitama	14.5	+20
Kyowa	13.2	+9
Hokkaido–Takushoku	9.6	+3

Notes:
[1] Year end March 31st, 1984
Source: Company Reports

City code. A published set of rules, first laid down in 1968, which must be followed by British PUBLIC COMPANIES and their advisers when bidding for (or resisting a bid from) another company. The TAKEOVER PANEL is responsible for seeing that the rules are obeyed.

Clearing bank. Those British banks that participate in Britain's CLEARING SYSTEMS. England and Scotland have separate clearing systems. The members of the English one are called the London clearing banks; the members of the Scottish one (straightforwardly) are the Scottish clearing banks.

Clearing house. The place where financial transactions (like SECURITIES and FUTURES sales, or bank payments) are docked off one ACCOUNT and credited to another. At a clearing house, payments among active financial institutions can be NETTED out against each other at the end of a day, thereby reducing the number of entries needed in their books.

Clearing House Automated Payment System (CHAPS). A scheme to automate London's TOWN CLEARING. It enables payments of over £10,000 to be made instantly by computer rather than by the hand of a CITY messenger (as in the town clearing) or over a period of days. First mooted in the mid-1970s, it finally came into operation on 9 February 1984 to a fanfare of indifference. All but the very biggest banks found it expensive.

Clearing House Interbank Payment System (CHIPS). The New York near-equivalent of (and predecessor to) London's CLEARING HOUSE AUTOMATED PAYMENT SYSTEM: a computerized system of clearing big payments between financial institutions based in New York in one day. No one has yet invented FISH, the financial institutions' settlement house.

Clearing system. A system set up by a group of financial institutions for sorting out a large number of payments between themselves. The best known clearing systems are for sorting out cheques drawn on an account at one bank and owed to an account at another. But there are also clearing schemes for sorting out payments due on the sale of bonds (see CEDEL and EUROCLEAR).

Close company. A company in Britain controlled by fewer than six people. The company must also:
- Be resident in the United Kingdom.
- Have less than 35 per cent of its CAPITAL held by the public, and
- Not be controlled by another company that is not a close company.
  It then gets special treatment from the tax man.

Closed-end investment fund. The American expression for what in Britain is simply called an INVESTMENT TRUST. 'Closed-end' refers to the fact that there is a limited number of shares in the fund, unlike an OPEN-END INVESTMENT FUND (called UNIT TRUST in Britain). In the open-ended variety, new shares are issued every time an investor puts more money into the fund.

Clydesdale Bank. Smallest of the three main Scottish CLEARING BANKS (the BANK OF SCOTLAND and the ROYAL BANK OF SCOTLAND are bigger), Clydesdale has been the most innovative in the use of new technology. Sometimes it has been more innovative than the giant English banks, even though one of them (the MIDLAND) owns it.

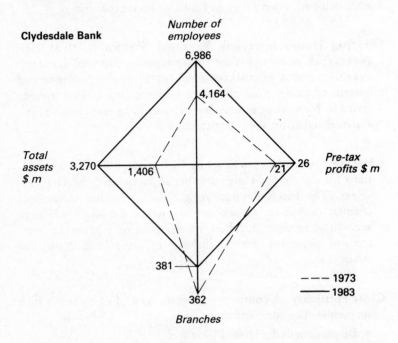

Clydesdale Bank

Number of employees

6,986

4,164

Total assets $ m   3,270   1,406   21   26   Pre-tax profits $ m

381

362

Branches

----- 1973
——— 1983

COFACE. France's EXPORT CREDIT insurance agency. COFACE (short for Compagnie Française d'Assurance pour le Commerce Extérieur) is a company owned jointly by the state, nationalized banks and insurance companies. It provides insurance cover for

commercial risks on export credits of up to three years' MATUR-
ITY. For commercial risks on loans with a longer maturity and
for political risks it also provides cover – but only acting as agent
for the state.

Co-financing. The joint financing of projects in developing countries by the WORLD BANK and A. N. Other. (A. N. Other can be a
COMMERCIAL BANK, a government or an EXPORT CREDIT agency.)
Co-financing can benefit everybody. It helps the World Bank to
direct more money to developing countries than its own resources allow. And it gives governments and commercial banks
the comfort of knowing that borrowers almost never DEFAULT on
loans involving the World Bank.

Since the first co-financing experiment in 1974, there have
been over 800 such schemes, involving about $36 billion. BANK
OF AMERICA was the leading commercial bank in the field until its
managing director, Mr Tom Clausen, went to head up the
World Bank. His enthusiasm has not waned in his new job, but
co-financing has been held back by its complexity. Inextricably
intertwining many different lenders is a legal nightmare.

Coin. A piece of metal with a value and (sometimes) the face of
somebody important stamped on it. Britain's lowest denomination coin, the halfpenny, is to disappear at the end of 1984.

Collateral. For all intents and purposes, the same as SECURITY.

Comecon. The popular name for the Council for Mutual Economic Assistance (CMEA). A sort of communist EEC founded in
1949 to coordinate the economic development of its member
states, viz. Eastern Europe, Cuba, Mongolia, Vietnam and the
Soviet Union.

Commercial bank. Those banks that are most visible to the
general public. Their main business is taking in deposits and
making loans to individuals and industry – a business that they
conduct through a network of branches. They are commercial in
two senses: they make loans to commerce (ie, for the financing of
trade) and they are themselves commercial profit-oriented
businesses.

Table 9 *The 20 biggest commercial banks by assets[1]*

	Country	Assets ($b)	
		1983	1982
Citibank	US	126	121
Bank of America	US	115	115
Dai-Ichi Kangyo	Japan	110	87
Fuji	Japan	103	84
Sumitomo	Japan	101	81
Banque Nationale de Paris	France	101	110
Mitsubishi	Japan	98	81
Crédit Lyonnais	France	97	97
Barclays	Britain	94	95
Sanwa	Japan	91	75
Crédit Agricole	France	90	99
National Westminster	Britain	87	88
Société Générale	France	86	86
Chase Manhattan	US	82	81
Norinchukin	Japan	81	60
Deutsche	W. Germany	77	83
Midland	Britain	76	77
Industrial Bank of Japan	Japan	71	60
Mitsui	Japan	69	57
Bank of Tokyo	Japan	67	64

Note:
[1] end-year
Source: Euromoney

Table 10 *The 20 biggest commercial banks by equity[1]*

	Total shareholders/ funds $b	Net Income $m	Number of employees
Citibank	5.23	860	63,700
Bank of America	4.34	390	91,100
Barclays	4.29	419	123,000
National Westminster	4.17	574	88,000
Crédit Agricole	4.02	194	72,800
Banco do Brasil	3.33	498	117,000
Lloyds	3.18	400	69,300
Fuji[2]	3.08	269	17,200
J. P. Morgan	3.07	460	13,000
Chase Manhattan	3.05	430	37,200

Table 10 *cont.*

Sumitomo	2.99	295	13,800
Dai-Ichi Kangyo[2]	2.91	181	22,800
Mitsubishi[2]	2.77	195	18,300
Midland	2.75	171	82,600
Union Bank of Switzerland	2.70	232	17,200
Sanwa[2]	2.53	180	16,600
Deutsche	2.52	240	47,300
Hongkong and Shanghai Banking Corporation	2.52	320	45,000
Swiss Bank Corporation	2.41	197	14,300
First Interstate	2.28	260	29,000

Notes:
[1] end 1983   [2] September 30th, 1983
Source: Euromoney

Commercial bill. A BILL OF EXCHANGE which finances a SHORT-TERM self-liquidating commercial transaction, like the export of goods.

Commercial paper. Not a collective noun for the *Wall Street Journal,* and the *Financial Times,* but SHORT-TERM debt instruments issued by American companies or banks. Commercial paper has a MATURITY of from five to 270 days (most frequently between thirty and ninety days), and is usually issued in dollops of $100,000. In the United States, at the end of October, 1983, there was $177 billion worth of commercial paper in circulation. In December, 1970, there was only $33.5 billion worth. Financial companies account for about 70 per cent of the paper issued.

Commerzbank. West Germany's third biggest bank often in the shadow of the two Ds (DEUTSCHE BANK and DRESDNER BANK). Like the two Ds. Commerzbank is a UNIVERSAL BANK. In recent years its performance has been much worse than that of its rivals. In 1980 its profit slumped to DM 18 million from DM 155 million in 1979. It paid no dividend for three years and was forced to sell its Frankfurt head office and lease it back from the buyer.

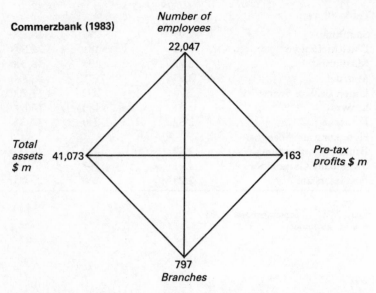

Commerzbank (1983)

Number of employees 22,047

Total assets $ m 41,073

Pre-tax profits $ m 163

Branches 797

Commission. The reward of an agent; the amount he adds on to the price of the transaction that he carries out on behalf of a client.

Commitment fee. Payment for promises. A fee paid by a potential borrower to his bank to extract a promise of a bank loan when he wants it. The fee is usually a fraction of 1 per cent of the amount committed.

Committee of London Clearing Bankers (CLCB). The exclusive club of English (i.e. not Scottish) CLEARING BANKS. The actual members of the CLCB are the chairmen of six banks BARCLAYS, the NATIONAL WESTMINSTER, the MIDLAND, LLOYDS, Williams & Glyn's and COUTTS), who meet regularly to discuss matters of common interest. Underneath the committee itself are various other committees which discuss things like tax, electronic gadgetry and banking law.

The CLCB banks are the main participants in the CHEQUE CLEARING SYSTEM and act as agents for outsider banks who would like to join. They have opened their clearing doors a little bit to let the Bank of England, the Co-operative Bank, the government's National Girobank and the Central Trustee Savings Bank into the system. The group has also received applications to join from the American CITICORP (the first foreigner to apply) and Standard Chartered. Qualifications for entry include a branch network, a CITY office, 1 per cent of the volume of cheques cleared and/or a face that fits.

Compensating balance. When a company borrows from a bank it may be asked by the bank to keep a certain amount in a DEPOSIT ACCOUNT with the bank. Sounds absurd? Why borrow so much if you've still got something to leave in the bank? Good question, difficult to answer. Probably to make effective lending RATES higher than the legal limits. Anyway, compensating balances (which increase the total cost of borrowing) are very common in the United States and Japan.

Compensatory financing facility. A special fund set up by the INTERNATIONAL MONETARY FUND to help member countries with BALANCE OF PAYMENTS problems caused by temporary falls in the price of basic commodities (like copper or tin) that they export and on which they are largely dependent. Since May, 1981, the facility has also been available to countries that have balance of payments problems from erratic movements in the price of staple cereal imports.

Competition and credit control. A new way of regulating banks introduced in Britain in 1971. It replaced direct controls on bank lending with a package of measures including a RESERVE RATIO requirement common to all banks.

Composite rate. The peculiar way in which tax is paid on BUILD-ING SOCIETY depositors' INTEREST. The depositors receive their interest after tax has been withheld at the basic RATE (30 per cent). The societies then pay over tax on the depositors' behalf, not at the basic rate but at the composite rate, currently 25 per cent. This takes into account the fact that some (around 17 per cent) of building societies' deposits belong to non-taxpayers.

The invidious effect of the composite rate is that taxpayers are subsidized by non-taxpayers because non-taxpayers cannot re-claim from the Inland Revenue the tax withheld on their behalf. This gross injustice is perpetrated in the name of efficiency. It takes fewer tax collectors to gather the composite rate from building societies than to collect tax due from every individual saver. So compelling is this attraction that Britain's government is to extend the system to bank deposits.

Comptroller of the Currency. One of the regulators in America's tangled web of bank REGULATION. The Comptroller, an official of the US Treasury and based in Washington DC, is responsible for supervising banks with a national (as opposed to a state) charter. In the 1950s national banks began to set up bank holding companies (companies that own one or more banks). The bank holding companies can do non-banking business prohibited to banks. The task of supervising these holding companies was handed to the FEDERAL RESERVE BOARD.

The two regulators have sometimes come into conflict, not only with each other but also with the state superintendents who oversee the STATE CHARTERED BANKS. Banks sometimes play off one regulator against another, switching from a state to a national charter (or vice versa) if they think they can get permission for something from one but not the other.

In 1984, a committee under the chairmanship of vice-president GEORGE BUSH came up with suggestions for ways in which America's complicated system of regulation could be simplified.

Concert party. Nothing to do with the Royal Albert Hall. A group of investors who act in concert to try to gain control of a company. Each buys a small stake, all of which, when combined, amount to a controlling interest.

Concordat. A secret agreement among CENTRAL BANKERS thrashed out in 1975 at the BANK FOR INTERNATIONAL SETTLEMENTS in Basel, Switzerland, and sometimes referred to as the Basel Concordat. The overriding aim of the agreement was to ensure that no part of international banks' activities was left unsupervised. In general, two methods have been used to achieve this aim: greater co-operation and exchanges of information amongst national bank supervisors, and more consolidated accounting of banks' businesses worldwide. The Concordat was revised and published in 1983 after BANCO AMBROSIANO had shown it to be full of holes.

Confidence. The quality that keeps banks in business. If a bank's depositors did not have confidence that the bank could repay them their deposits whenever they wanted, their fears would be self-fulfilling. If they all rushed to withdraw their deposits at the same time, the bank would then, indeed, not be able to repay them. Banks use other people's fears of a loss of confidence to cover a multitude of sins – particularly in their perpetual desire to disclose as little information to the public as possible (see SEC-RECY). As the *Wall Street Journal* once put it: 'It is a truism that confidence is important to banks. That is why the early Hebrews did their banking in temples and the later Americans and Europeans built banks that looked like temples'.

Consensus. Short for the 'International Agreement for Guidelines on Officially Supported Export Credit', an agreement between twenty-two ORGANIZATION FOR ECONOMIC CO-OPERATION AND DEVELOPMENT member countries on how far they will go in subsidizing INTEREST RATES on loans to their exporters. All twenty-two countries have official EXPORT CREDIT agencies (like Britain's EXPORT CREDITS GUARANTEE DEPARTMENT).

The latest consensus is that the minimum rates of interest should be:

Table 11 *Consensus minimum interest rates (%)*

Borrower Terms	Relatively rich more than (US $4,000)[1]	Intermediate (US $625– 4,000)[1]	Relatively poor (under US $625)[1]
2–5 years	13.35	11.55	10.7
Over 5 years	13.6	11.9	10.7

Note: [1] GNP per capita in 1979

Consolidation. The combining of the accounts of a parent company with those of its subsidiaries. Only in Britain and the USA is there a long history of consolidation. For banks in continental Europe, consolidation is the exception rather than the rule. However, in West Germany, where the troubles of banks like Schroder, Munchmeyer Hengst were disguised by the non-consolidation of subsidiaries (particularly those in LUXEMBOURG), there are now moves to make consolidation compulsory.

Consortium bank. A bank owned by a group of other banks from a number of different countries, no one of which owns a majority share. Consortium banks were children of the EUROMARKET. Born in the 1970s they gave smaller banks a way into the Euromarket hand in hand with bigger bank partners. The advantage to the bigger banks lay in their easier access to the big domestic customers of the smaller banks.

The consortium banks' *raison d'être* has now diminished. Smaller banks want to be in the Euromarket on their own or not at all. Some consortium banks continue to thrive by staying at the forefront of new financing techniques, acting as a type of fleet-footed MERCHANT BANK, more flexible than any of their shareholders can be. Nevertheless, several consortium banks have been gobbled up recently by one or other of their shareholders. At the end of 1983 there were twenty-eight consortium banks in London.

Consumer credit. A bank loan to a consumer to enable him to consume the sorts of things you buy in shops and car showrooms. In Britain, the Consumer Credit Act of 1974 set out to protect consumers from being ripped off by loan sharks. Its main demand is that all providers of consumer credit indicate clearly to the borrower the real cost (the ANNUALIZED PERCENTAGE RATE) of his or her loan. In the United States, at least twelve different government agencies are involved in some way in ensuring that consumer credit is granted fairly.

Continental Illinois. Once the biggest bank in Chicago, Continental Illinois has now only one branch in its home state of Illinois, at its headquarters on Chicago's La Salle Street. The branch is more like a railway station than a branch.

Continental Illinois is famous for two other things: for being banker to the great swathe of Midwestern American industry, and for the losses it made on the energy loans passed to it by a peanut-sized bank in Oklahoma, PENN SQUARE. When Penn Square went bust in the middle of 1982, Continental Illinois made the biggest ever quarterly loss ($82.9 million) then recorded by an American bank.

These losses finally caught up with it in May 1984, when there was a RUN on the bank and it had to be bailed out by the FEDERAL DEPOSIT INSURANCE CORPORATION.

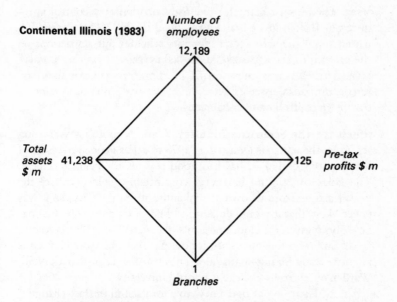

Continental Illinois (1983)

Number of employees 12,189

Total assets $ m 41,238

Pre-tax profits $ m 125

1 *Branches*

Contingent liability. A LIABILITY that becomes a liability only when something else happens. For example, a guarantor becomes liable for his GUARANTEE only if the debt that he has guaranteed does not get paid by the debtor.

Convertible bond. A BOND that can be exchanged for shares at a certain time at the request of the bond holder.

Co-operative bank. A bank that is run as a co-operative in which members buy shares. Their money is then used to make loans to other members: a sort of self-help institution. More common in continental Europe than in English-speaking countries.

Correspondent bank. In the old days, before banks started opening branches all over the world, they would make arrangements with other banks to act as their correspondents in foreign countries. When a bank's customers visited those countries (or did business there) the correspondent bank would provide services for them on behalf of their own bank back home. Although less significant now that so many banks are themselves multinational, correspondent banking is still an important part of banking business.

Corset. The popular name for one form of monetary control introduced in Britain in 1973 and abandoned in 1981. The corset (full-name: supplementary special deposits scheme) put restrictions on the growth of the COMMERCIAL BANKS' INTEREST – bearing ELIGIBLE LIABILITIES. Whereas most forms of monetary control focus on restricting banks' asset growth, the corset was unusual in concentrating on controlling their liabilities.

Council for the Securities Industry (CSI). A toothless watchdog set up by the BANK OF ENGLAND in 1978 to act as general overseer of the CITY of London. It has had good reasons for being toothless. The Bank of England has never comfortably yielded any of the power arising from its own special authority in the City, so it was never likely that it would do so to a child of its own. The CSI has never been given the clout to do an authoritative job. Until recently it had only two full-time staff; it now has six. The Council itself is twenty-strong (or not-so-strong). The chairman is Sir Patrick Neill, Warden of All Souls College, Oxford University.

The CSI is trying to find a new role for itself in the fast-changing British SECURITIES industry. If it fails, its demise could see the end of non-statutory outside regulation of the City. The CSI is the only forum in which non-City folk get a say in regulation. Of the twenty on the Council, three are lay members (i.e. ordinary investors and savers).

Counterfoil. The perforated slip attached to a CHEQUE. On it are written the details of the cheque (to whom it was payable, for how much and when). It enables the cheque writer to keep a record of his transactions.

Countertrade. See BARTER.

Country risk. A phenomenon rediscovered by banks during their splurge of international cross-border landing in the 1970s. When a bank in country A lends to a company in country B, it bears a risk that does not exist when it lends to a company in country A: the risk that country B will not provide the company with the necessary foreign exchange to repay the loan, even though the company itself is perfectly SOLVENT and willing to repay. As banks became more aware of the dangers of country risk, some began to employ political scientists to measure the immeasurable for them.

Coupon. A piece of paper attached to BEARER BONDS or SECURITIES which, when presented to the paying agent, gives the presenter the right to underlying DIVIDENDS or INTEREST due on the security.

Coutts & Co. A wholly owned subsidiary of NATIONAL WESTMINSTER BANK and smallest of the London CLEARING BANKS. Coutts retains old-world customs to please its old-world customers. Its male staff wear frock coats, and until 1955 it sent all its customers (who include most of the British royal family) hand-written STATEMENTS of their ACCOUNTS. Royals still get hand-written statements.

Coutts has only thirteen branches located in places like Eton and London's swish Park Lane and Mayfair. Its headquarters are in one of London's most famous landmarks – the pepperpot buildings on the Strand. The bank's chairman is the nicely named David Money-Coutts.

Crash. What happens when a lot of banks go bust at the same time. The last real crash the world has seen was in 1929. Since then, touch wood, crashes have all been figments of novelists' imaginations.

Crédit Agricole. The massive French CO-OPERATIVE BANK that sometimes lays claim to being the biggest bank in the world. Known as the Green bank, Crédit Agricole has traditionally been banker to French farmers – a powerful lobby that has ensured that it does not land Crédit Agricole with too many bad debts. (See diamond p. 48).

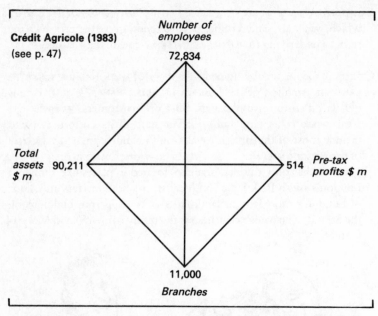

Crédit Agricole (1983)
(see p. 47)

Number of employees
72,834

Total assets $ m 90,211

Pre-tax profits $ m 514

11,000
Branches

Credit card. A plastic card that enables the holder not only to buy goods and services but also to buy them on credit. Most credit cards are issued by banks. Some are provided by retailers themselves. Two organizations, VISA and MASTERCARD, attempt to turn nationally recognized credit cards into internationally acceptable methods of payment. Credit cards are one of the fastest growing areas for bank fraud. In 1983 losses in Britain from plastic fraud were more than £30 million.

Table 12 *Credit Cards*

UK Credit Cards – 1983	Access	Visa
Number of cards issued	6.82 m	8.99 m
Value of turnover	£3.15 b	£3.22 b
Number of British outlets	205,000	202,000

Worldwide Credit Cards – 1984	Number of cards issued
Visa	105 m
Mastercard/Eurocard/Access	80 m
American Express	18 m
Diners Club	4 m

Credit line. What businessmen hang their hopes on – the amount of credit they can get banks to promise to give them when and if they need it.

Crédit Lyonnais. One of the big three French banks that were nationalized long before M. Mitterrand came to power and swept almost all the rest of French banking into the state sector. To foreigners the big three French banks are almost indistinguishable.

Crédit Lyonnais (1983) *Number of employees*

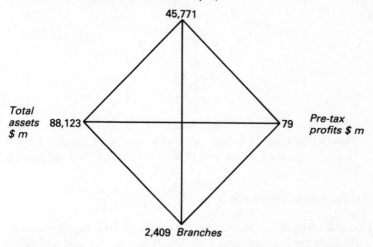

Crédit Suisse. Third of the big three Swiss banks (the others are UNION BANK OF SWITZERLAND and SWISS BANK CORPORATION), Crédit Suisse is a UNIVERSAL BANK occupying, along with the other two, a position of power within the economy of Switzerland not enjoyed by banks anywhere other than in HONGKONG. (See diamond p. 50.)

In 1977 Crédit Suisse suffered a blow when the manager of its Chiasso branch overreached his authority and lumbered the bank with some enormous losses. These were put at around SwFr 1.7 billion – an amount that Crédit Suisse managed to absorb from its vast HIDDEN RESERVES without causing a hiccough in it annual profits.

Credit union. An organization in which a group of people with a common bond (e.g. membership of the same club, trade union or sex) get together to pool their savings. They then lend out these savings to each other. Recent legislation attempted to encourage the

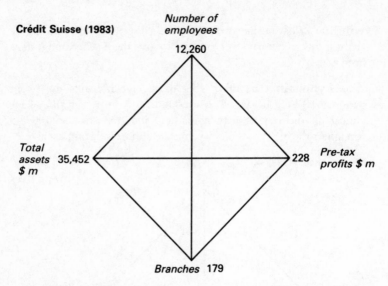

Crédit Suisse (1983)

Number of employees 12,260

Total assets $ m 35,452

Pre-tax profits $ m 228

Branches 179

growth of credit unions in Britain. So far, however, they have achieved nothing like their popularity in Canada or the United States, where there are almost 19,000 credit unions with total assets of over $100 billion.

Crédits mixtes. See MIXED CREDITS.

Crossed cheque. A cheque with two parallel lines drawn across it. Between the lines are written the words '& Co.' (or 'and company') or nothing. A crossed cheque must be paid into a bank ACCOUNT (any account will do). That makes it much less attractive to thieves than an OPEN CHEQUE, which can be exchanged for CASH.

Cum div. The opposite of EX DIV. A share that is being sold together with a DIVIDEND payment that has been declared but not yet distributed.

Cum rights. The opposite of EX RIGHTS. A share that is being sold together with the option to take up a RIGHTS ISSUE that has been announced but not yet completed.

Current account. The British expression for the Americans' checking account, (normally) a non-INTEREST-bearing account with a bank on which CHEQUES can be drawn and from which CASH can be taken on demand. (See also BALANCE OF PAYMENTS.)

D

Dai-Ichi Kangyo Bank (DKB). The biggest of Japan's CITY BANKS – the all-round COMMERCIAL BANKS that are the heart of the country's banking system. DKB has the biggest branch network in Japan with 345 offices (not many when you compare it with British banks). It has the second biggest international network after the BANK OF TOKYO.

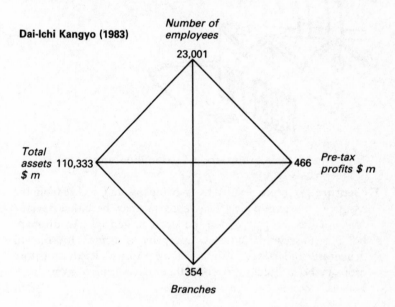

Dai-Ichi Kangyo (1983)

Dawn Raid. The takeover tactic of buying (in Britain) up to 29.9 per cent of a company (the maximum allowed before a full take-over bid must be launched) early one morning before the stock-market has opened. BROKERS get prior commitments to sell from investors, so that the whole thing is wrapped up before the stockmarket can catch a speculative whiff that someone is building up a stake in the company.

Famous dawn raids include the purchase by the West German insurance company Allianz of 29.9 per cent of Eagle Star, and the Australian company Bell Resources' 29.9 per cent stake in the entertainments group ACC. Bell successfully took over its prey. Allianz didn't. But weep not: Allianz eventually sold its stake to

BAT, the tobacco group, for a £166 million profit.

Debenture. A BOND issued by a company and secured on the ASSETS of the company. The SECURITY may be either specific assets of the company or all the assets in general. An ordinary bond is unsecured. When a company is being LIQUIDATED, debenture holders have a right to the company's leftovers before ordinary bond holders. Both of them have priority over shareholders.

Debit card. A plastic card which, when used in an AUTOMATED TELLER MACHINE or point-of-sale terminal (see EFTPOS), identifies the holder of a bank DEPOSIT ACCOUNT and debits the account with whatever money the cardholder authorizes. Unlike a CREDIT CARD, a debit card does not necessarily provide the card holder with credit facilities.

Debt–equity ratio. The ratio of a company's loans to its EQUITY (shareholders' funds). (See GEARING.)

Debt service ratio. The ratio of a country's repayments on its foreign debt to its HARD-CURRENCY export earnings. Many different ratios can be calculated depending on which repayments are included – e.g. INTEREST and PRINCIPAL; interest only; LONG-TERM and SHORT-TERM debt; or long-term only. Bankers use the ratios as crucial guides to a country's creditworthiness. Unfortunately, by the time the ratios have been calculated to be horrendous, the country is often already desperately RESCHEDULING its debts.

Too much attention to debt service ratios can be unhealthy for another reason. Most countries' first call on their hard-currency export earnings is for buying vital imports, not for repaying bank loans.

Table 13 *Debt service ratios 1983*

Interest Payments[1]		Total Debt Repayments[1]	
Brazil	42.6	Argentina	173.6
Argentina	32.1	Brazil	149.2
Chile	28.1	Mexico	141.2
Mexico	27.9	Philippines	131.3
Philippines	27.6	Sudan	121.8
Morocco	27.6	Peru	121.6
Sudan	27.4	Venezuela	107.1
Ecuador	24.7	Ecuador	103.8
Peru	21.9	Chile	100.7
Ivory Coast	21.7	Morocco	94.2

Note:
[1] as a percentage of foreign exchange earnings

Default. The failure to repay a loan on schedule. Once a borrower is in default there are certain legal moves his bank can make to try to recover its money or to get hold of the underlying SECURITY backing its loan.

Defaults happen every day without causing too much stir. Bankers' biggest fear is that one black Friday Brazil, Argentina and Mexico will all default at the same time. That would bring the end of the world's banking system as we know it.

Defeasance. A technique whereby big companies can borrow money without showing it on their balance sheets. A company borrows the money and uses most of it to buy enough government SECURITIES in the same currency to ensure that the income from the securities is sufficient to match the servicing costs of the borrowing. The securities and the borrowing are wrapped up in a trust. Hey presto, it all comes off the balance sheet and, if the company is popular enough (i.e. if it can borrow more cheaply than the country whose government securities it has bought), it is left with a profit at the end.

Deposit account. A bank ACCOUNT against which CHEQUES cannot be drawn and which must always be kept in credit. INTEREST is paid on the balance in a deposit account. CASH can be withdrawn from the account if sufficient notice is given (in theory, usually seven days; in practice, often on demand).

Deposit Protection Board. The body set up in Britain under the 1979 BANKING ACT to administer the banks' DEPOSIT PROTECTION FUND.

Deposit protection fund. A fund set up to reassure depositors that, should the financial institution of their choice go bust, they will get some of their money back. A deposit protection fund is sometimes a legal requirement (as for banks in Britain under the 1979 BANKING ACT) and sometimes a voluntary system set up by an association of deposit-takers (such as the one for Britain's BUILDING SOCIETIES).

Protection for depositors is not always provided by the existence of an actual fund of money on which they have a claim should their bank go bust. It can be set up simply as a form of GUARANTEE under which institutions promise to cough up should the need arise or, as in the United States, as an insurance scheme (the FEDERAL DEPOSIT INSURANCE CORPORATION) to which the participating institutions pay a PREMIUM.

Depository Institutions Deregulation and Monetary Control Act. A 1980 piece of American legislation designed to phase out INTEREST-RATE controls on banks and THRIFTS. The process, to be spread over a number of years, is overseen by a committee, the Depository Institutions Deregulation Committee (DIDC). On the DIDC sit representatives of the many agencies in America charged with bank and thrift regulation.

Depreciation. The amount by which an ASSET's value is reduced because it is wasting away – for instance, a bank branch that is owned on a long lease will be worth less and less (in real terms) as the years go by.

Deregulation. The process of removing legal or quasi-legal restrictions on the types of business done or the prices charged within a particular industry. In Britain, the United States and Japan, the financial industry is currently being deregulated. In the United States, price controls (i.e. interest-rate ceilings – see REGULATION Q) have been removed. In Britain, banks are being allowed to become STOCKBROKERS.

Deutsche Bank. The biggest and (maybe) the best COMMERCIAL BANK in West Germany. While its rivals have suffered blows from over-lending to places like Poland and to troubled West German companies like AEG, Deutsche has marched on from profit to profit. In celebration, it is building itself a new twin-tower extravaganza for its head office that promises to be the showpiece of Frankfurt, West Germany's financial capital.

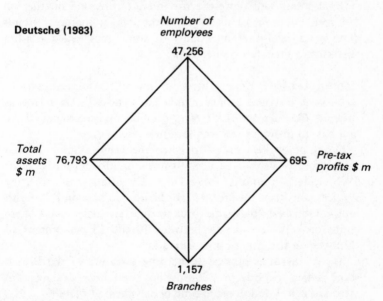

Deutsche (1983)

Number of employees
47,256

Total assets $ m   76,793

695   Pre-tax profits $ m

1,157
Branches

Like other big West German banks, Deutsche is a UNIVERSAL BANK doing almost every conceivable thing a bank can do, including taking big EQUITY stakes in West German industry.

Deutsche has more than forty overseas offices and is one of the busiest banks in both the Euroloan and the EUROBOND business.

The bank, founded in Berlin in 1870, now has over 1,300 offices inside Germany, 45,000 employees and 240,000 shareholders.

Devaluation. A government-directed downward jerk in the value of its currency *vis-à-vis* other currencies.

Direct debit. An instruction from a bank's customer telling the bank to debit his ACCOUNT with the amount demanded by a named creditor. Direct debits are designed to make it easy to pay regular but varying bills (like those for gas and electricity) with a minimum of fuss. Trouble is, customers do not like them, since direct debits take control of their cash flow out of their hands.

Discount. Two meanings: to sell at a reduced price, or the reduction in price itself. In financial markets discounting is common; a banker may sell a bill at a discount to its FACE VALUE. The discount will represent the interest foregone on the bill between the time of its sale and the date it matures. Bonds (known as deep-discount bonds) are sometimes issued at a big discount to their face value.

Discount broker. A new breed of no-frills American STOCK-BROKER. A discount broker simply buys and sells SECURITIES as ordered. He does no UNDERWRITING, offers no investment advice and has no in-house research facilities.

Discount brokers grew up when the United States moved from fixed to negotiated COMMISSIONS for brokers on 30 April 1975 (called, ironically, May Day). By offering no ancillary services, the discount brokers are able to compete on price with long-established, big-name brokers like MERRILL LYNCH. Discount brokers now handle between 10 and 15 per cent of all turnover on the American stockmarkets.

Expect discount brokers to become a feature of the British scene when negotiated commissions on share dealings are introduced in London some time before the end of 1986.

Discount house. Unnecessary go-between imposed on the banking system by the BANK OF ENGLAND to distribute Britain's MONEY

SUPPLY to the MONEY MARKETS. Every workday morning employees of the discount houses don top hats and set out on their rounds of the CITY of London's big banks. Their aim is to find out if the banks are short of CASH (they usually are these days). The houses then get some for them by selling BILLS to the Bank of England.

Table 14 *Discount Houses*

	Total assets		Net profit		Year end
	1983	1984	1983	1984	
		(£ b)		(£ m)	
Gerrard & National	2.56	3.52	14.21	10.11	5 Apr
Union Discount	2.23	1.80	11.37	6.12	1 Jan
Cater Allen Holdings	1.13	1.44	4.25	4.80	30 Apr
Alexanders Discount	0.63	0.82	3.00	2.25	1 Jan
Jessel, Toynbee & Gillett					
King & Shaxson	0.62	0.61	2.17	1.66	5 Apr
Smith St Aubyn	0.48	0.50	1.50	1.10	30 Apr
Clive Discount	0.42	0.42	1.42	2.51	5 Apr
Seccombe Marshall & Campion	0.39	0.44	1.85	1.26	31 Mar
Gerald Quin, Cope	0.17	0.18	0.43	0.49	30 Apr
Page & Gwyther	0.05	—	(0.06)[1]	—	30 Jan
	0.04	—	0.09	—	—

[1] 1982 (latest available year)
Source: Company reports

Discount market. The markets in SHORT-TERM financial instruments made by Britain's ten DISCOUNT HOUSES. Through these markets the BANK OF ENGLAND fine-tunes the nation's MONEY SUPPLY. Although the size of the discount market has increased rapidly in recent years, the number of players in the market (the discount houses) has dwindled. Smaller houses have merged as the Bank of England's modifications of monetary policy have favoured the biggest.

Two houses, Gerrard & National and Union Discount, now account for 50–60 per cent of the market. Whereas twenty years ago much of the discount market's business was in TREASURY

BILLS, it now deals in a wider range of short-term ASSETS – in particular, bank BILLS and CERTIFICATES OF DEPOSIT. Treasury bills rarely account for more than 2 per cent of all the discount houses' assets.

Discount rate. The INTEREST RATE at which CENTRAL BANKS will DISCOUNT government and other first-class debt instruments from COMMERCIAL BANKS, or the rate at which they will lend to banks with the instruments as COLLATERAL.

Discount window. The 'window' at the federal reserve banks of the United States where banks may borrow SHORT-TERM (at the DISCOUNT RATE) to help them make an orderly adjustment to sudden unexpected changes in their loans (ASSETS) or deposits (LIABILITIES). The MATURITY of loans from the discount window rarely exceeds two weeks. Smaller American banks can also borrow for rather longer periods under the SEASONAL BORROWING scheme.

Discounted cash flow. A method of calculating the present value of a string of payments in the future. Say you are to receive £100 in one year's time. If you had the £100 now, you could invest it and earn, say, 8 per cent INTEREST. So with around £92 you could have £100 at the end of the year. The discounted cash flow value (see CAPITALIZED VALUE) of your yet-to-be received £100 is, therefore, about £92.

Disintermediation. Buzz word meaning the exclusion of financial institutions (like banks) from the process of allocating savings. Disintermediation can happen in several ways: for example, companies can come to rely on BOND and EQUITY ISSUES rather than on bank loans; or governments can tap the personal sector's savings through the POST OFFICE system rather than by selling its bonds to banks.

Dividend. The reward of shareholders – that part of a company's profits paid out to its owners. The amount of dividend to be paid is announced at the company's annual general meeting but is often paid out in two instalments six months apart. The level of dividend payment is taken very seriously by public companies as a key indicator of their continuing success. (See EX-DIV and CUM-DIV.)

Documentary credits. A method of financing trade. Banks provide the buyer of goods with credit on the strength of documents which prove that the buyer has title to the goods. Useful when documents reach the buyer much more quickly than the goods themselves. More than half of all documentary credits lodged with banks by British companies get rejected because they arrive late or are incorrectly completed.

Domicile. A peculiar concept in British tax law that is gradually being written out of the tax books. 'Domicile' refers to the place where a person intends to live for the bulk of his life – essentially the place where he would like to lay his bones to rest.

People resident in Britain but not domiciled there pay much lower RATES of income tax if they work for foreign companies: they pay tax on 50 per cent of their income if they have been resident in Britain for fewer than nine out of the past ten years and on 75 per cent thereafter. The 1984 Finance Act introduced measures that will abolish these privileges by 1989.

Draft. Another word for BILL OF EXCHANGE.

Dresdner Bank. West Germany's second biggest bank (after DEUTSCHE BANK). Founded in 1872, it has 34,000 employees, 150,000 shareholders and 998 offices (forty-eight of them outside West Germany).

Like most German banks, it has a big subsidiary in LUXEMBOURG through which it does much of its EUROMARKET business. In recent years Dresdner has fallen on hard times because of too many loans to Poland and to the troubled electrical giant AEG. Its profits dropped from DM207 million in 1979 to DM139 million in 1981, the year it cut its DIVIDEND for the first time in decades – for a German bank, a terrible disgrace. See diamond p. 60.

Drysdale Government Securities. An American dealer in government SECURITIES that went belly-up in 1982, leaving America's third biggest bank, CHASE MANHATTAN, with some hefty losses. Chase had bankrolled much of the company's phenomenally fast growth.

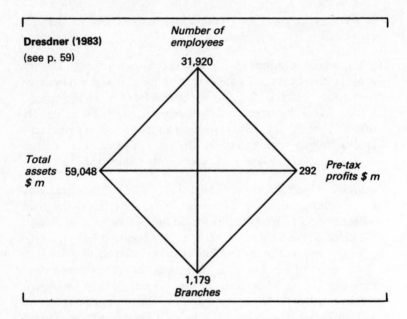

Dresdner (1983)
(see p. 59)

Number of employees

31,920

Total assets $ m   59,048

292   Pre-tax profits $ m

1,179
Branches

Drysdale became something of a *cause célèbre*. It gave the first indication of how risky is the unregulated SECONDARY MARKET in American government securities, and put the authorities in a dilemma. They were reluctant to tighten up the market too much for fear of making it even more difficult to sell the mountain of debt that their gaping budget deficit demanded.

Dual capacity. The ability of the same financial institution to be both STOCKBROKER (agent) and stock JOBBER (principal). The opposite of SINGLE CAPACITY.

Duncan, the Rev. Henry. The founder of the SAVINGS BANK movement. Born in 1774, he set up the first savings bank the world had ever seen – in a crofter's cottage at Ruthwell, Scotland, in 1810.

E

Edge Act. An American banking law passed in 1919 which first allowed American banks to do foreign business. In the early years of the Act that was limited to foreign trade financing, until then dominated by the British MERCHANT BANKS. After the Second World War the Americans got such an itch for Edge Act business that they spread all over the globe.

EFTPOS. A word to conjure with and one to watch. Short for 'Electronic Funds Transfer at the Point of Sale', EFTPOS is the way we will all pay for our shopping in the future. An electronic terminal at the shop's check-out point will read a plastic card from the customer's bank, automatically indicate whether there is enough money or credit in the ACCOUNT to meet the bill and, there and then, debit the amount with the cost of the goods.

EFTPOS will be nice for shopkeepers. They will be sure of being paid and of being paid soon. Customers might not like it so much, since it may debit their accounts earlier – no two- to three-day GRACE PERIOD as with a CHEQUE.

Egibi. A private bank in Damascus; probably the first bank in the world. Mr. Egibi, the bank's founder, lived in the latter part of the reign of the Babylonian King Sennacherib (705–681 BC). A stone tablet recording the bank's first loan is in the British Museum.

Eligible bank. A RECOGNIZED BANK in Britain whose sterling ACCEPTANCES are eligible for REDISCOUNT at the BANK OF ENGLAND. This was a privilege reserved until recently for the seventeen members of the ACCEPTING HOUSES COMMITTEE, plus a few British and White Commonwealth banks. Now there are more than 120 eligible banks, including many non-British ones.

Eligible liabilities. The deposits of banks in Britain that count towards their RESERVE RATIO, a lynchpin in the BANK OF ENGLAND's control of the banking system. The banks' eligible liabilities are their sterling deposits with an original MATURITY of less than two years, plus some other bits and pieces.

Endorsement. The signature on the back of a CHEQUE (or similar financial instrument) which transfers ownership of the instrument from the signatory to the bearer. A bearer instrument (such as an OPEN CHEQUE) does not need endorsement.

Equity. That part of a company's CAPITAL belonging to its shareholders. In a QUOTED COMPANY this is worth the price per share times the number of shares. On the company's balance sheet it is what is left over when all the company's LIABILITIES have been deducted from its ASSETS except those liabilities due to shareholders. In Britain, shares are themselves often referred to as equities.

Equity participation. Something that British and American banks have traditionally avoided and continental European banks have not: taking EQUITY stakes in their corporate customers. As British banks build up their MERCHANT BANK and VENTURE CAPITAL businesses, their equity participations are increasing.

Escrow account. A bank ACCOUNT kept by a third party on behalf of two others in dispute over its rightful ownership. The disputing parties try to set out conditions under which they will agree to let the money be released. When these conditions are met, the third party releases the funds. The most famous escrow account in recent years was the one set up to hold Iran's deposits with Western banks after the Shah's downfall.

Eurobonds – 1983: New Issues

by currency	no	value $ b
US dollar	292	35.15
Deutschmark	79	4.13
ECU	44	1.71
Pound	23	1.56
Canadian dollar	26	1.07
Yen	4	0.30
Australian dollar	8	0.22
Norwegian kroner	2	0.04
Kuwait dinar	1	0.02
NZ dollar	2	0.02
by type	346	26.50
Straights	71	12.87
FRNs	32	1.67
Convertible	30	3.02
Warrant	2	0.15
Zero Coupon	—	—
Exchange Options		

Source: Agefi.

Eurobond. A BOND, issued by a company or a government, with
two peculiar characteristics:

● It is issued in a market other than that of its currency of
denomination.

● The banks that issue it sell it internationally and not in just one
domestic market.

Hence, when West Germany's DEUTSCHE BANK issues a dollar
bond for Britain's ICI, which it then sells around the world, the
issue is a Eurobond.

Table 15   *Eurobonds – Lead managers, 1983*

	Total value $ b	Number of issues
Crédit Suisse – First Boston	9.78	51
Deutsche Bank	6.39	49
S. G. Warburg	2.00	28
Morgan Stanley	1.73	21
Morgan Guaranty	1.36	13
Merrill Lynch	1.32	11
Dresdner Bank	1.26	14
BNP	1.21	9
Goldman Sachs	1.03	11
Commerzbank	1.02	17

Source: Agefi

The Eurobond market has grown enormously in recent years. Turnover in the market is now reckoned to be greater than the combined turnover of the New York and London STOCK EXCHANGES. However, the market, having no one natural base, goes largely unrecorded and unregulated.

Eurocard. A European TRAVEL AND ENTERTAINMENT CARD developed to counteract the American dominance of the business. Eurocard is linked with MASTERCARD – but is still small.

Eurocheque. A uniform payments system being developed by European banks. It enables travellers around Europe to cash CHEQUES of up to the equivalent of SwFr 300 when backed by a standardized Eurocheque GUARANTEE card. They can draw cash from banks or pay by cheque in shops and hotels up to the same amount.

British banks have not yet fully joined the Eurocheque system, though MIDLAND BANK has begun to offer its customers Eurocheques. There is no denomination written on the cheques, and they are given out in small doses (twelve at a time).

Euroclear. A CLEARING SYSTEM for international BONDS run in Brussels by MORGAN GUARANTY on behalf of more than 100 banks that own it. In 1983 it cleared $604 billion worth of SECURITIES, up from $509 billion in 1982.

Eurodollar. Dollars held outside the United States. Legend has it that the first Eurodollar was created by the Russians, who were eager to own dollars but not eager to own them in America. So their dollars were kept in Europe and called Eurodollars.

After the Eurodollar came the Euroyen, the Euromark, the Eurofranc and the Euro-almost-anything-else-you-care-to-think-of. These huge pools of currency held outside their country of issue have grown fast (from about $600 billion worth in 1976 to about $2,000 billion worth at the end of 1983). They have given CENTRAL BANKERS palpitations, so far without justification.

In recent years Eurocurrencies have become less Eurocentric. Whereas in 1979 69 per cent were held in Western Europe, at the end of 1983 only 60 per cent were in Europe. The biggest gainer, ironically, was the United States, which in 1981 set up INTER-NATIONAL BANKING FACILITIES to lure Eurodollars back home.

Euromarket. A general word for the EUROBOND and Euroloan markets. Euroloans are loans of EURODOLLARS and of other Eurocurrencies.

Table 16 *The Euromarket's largest borrowers in 1983[1]*
(Eurobonds plus Euroloans)

	Total value $ b	Bonds $ b	Credits $ b
United States	28.57	8.61	19.96
Japan	15.40	14.09	1.31
Brazil	13.66	—	13.66
Mexico	13.02	—	13.02
Canada	11.31	7.10	4.21
France	10.29	6.88	3.41
Australia	8.57	1.69	6.88
Spain	6.49	1.35	5.14
Sweden	6.02	3.76	2.26
Italy	5.66	1.44	4.22

Note:
[1] by country of origin of borrower
Source: Agefi

European currency unit (ECU). An artificial currency rather like SPECIAL DRAWING RIGHTS (SDR). The ECU is based on a basket of European currencies. It is proving more popular for commercial transactions than the SDR because it does not try to cover every major currency in the world. It is now possible to open a bank ACCOUNT in ECUs and to buy ECU traveller's cheques. There is also a healthy ECU-denominated sector of the EUROBOND market.

European Economic Community (EEC). Formed by the Treaty of Rome in 1957. Its six original member countries (Belgium, France, the Netherlands, Italy, LUXEMBOURG and West Germany) have since been joined by four others (Britain,

Denmark, Greece and Ireland). The Community's aim is to establish the free movement of capital, labour and services throughout the member states – an aim that is more easily stated than achieved.

European Free Trade Association (EFTA). A sort of compensation prize for Western European countries who could not (or did not want to) get into the EUROPEAN ECONOMIC COMMUNITY (EEC). EFTA was set up in 1960 by Britain, Denmark, Austria, Norway, Sweden, Switzerland and Portugal. They were later joined by Iceland and Finland. Britain and Denmark left EFTA in 1972 prior to joining the EEC.

The aim of EFTA is to reduce tariffs on trade between member countries so that their industries will not be squeezed out of Europe by giant traders within the EEC.

European Investment Bank (EIB). A Euro-invention established by the Treaty of Rome in 1957. The EIB acts as a development bank for Europe – i.e. a bank that uses its good reputation to borrow cheaply in international CAPITAL MARKETS in order to lend to borrowers within the EUROPEAN ECONOMIC COMMUNITY (EEC) and to its associate members. Most EIB loans are for terms of between seven and twelve years. At the end of 1983 it had lent 24.6 billion EUROPEAN CURRENCY UNITS.

The bank has certain priorities. It favours lending:
● To depressed areas like Northern Ireland and the Mezzogiorno.
● For the development of European technology.
● For infrastructure projects that involve more than one member country of the EEC – like the Channel Tunnel.
● For projects that further a particular interest of the Community.

European Monetary System (EMS). A scheme to manage the way in which eight European currencies FLOAT against each other. The EMS started on 13 March 1979 as the successor of the 'snake', the first international attempt to dampen wilder fluctuations in exchange RATES after the dollar had been allowed to float freely in 1971.

Membership of the EMS is voluntary. Britain is out of it; Ireland is in.

Euro-Treasuries. One of the EUROBOND market's more exotic inventions – a security which entitles the holder to buy a particular US Treasury BOND at a fixed price and at any time within a given period.

Ex div. A sort of *nota bene* added to the quoted price of shares to indicate that the shares are being offered exclusive of a DIVIDEND payment that is about to be made.

Ex new (or ex rights). A little note (like EX DIV) next to a share price to indicate that the share is being sold without the benefit of a RIGHTS ISSUE that has been announced but not yet taken up.

Exchange Equalization Account. An ACCOUNT held by Britain's Treasury at the BANK OF ENGLAND. In it are kept all the country's gold and foreign currency RESERVES. The Bank dips into the account if it wishes to support sterling's exchange RATE. By using the foreign currency to buy sterling in the foreign exchange market, it keeps the pound's exchange rate higher than it would otherwise be.

Eximbank. The agency in the United States which gives GUARANTEES and insurance for EXPORT CREDITS. Unlike its counterparts in Europe, Eximbank is more than just a specialized insurance company. It is also a bank which lends more than $3 billion a year to finance American exports.

Export credit. A loan to an exporter to tide him over the time between sending his goods abroad and receiving payment for them from the importer. For exports of large CAPITAL GOODS that can be several years.

Export Credits Guarantee Department (ECGD). Britain's EXPORT CREDIT agency, designed to persuade foreigners to spend more than they can afford and to spend it in Britain. ECGD is a government department that lends no money. It insures exporters against loss and gives banks GUARANTEES that their export credits will be repaid. It also gives INTEREST-RATE subsidies on MEDIUM-TERM, FIXED-RATE export credits. The subsidy is the difference between a rate set by ORGANIZATION FOR ECONOMIC CO-

OPERATION AND DEVELOPMENT countries in the CONSENSUS and market rates.

Ever since developing countries like Nigeria had difficulty repaying their debts on time, ECGD has been coughing up rather a lot. In 1983 it made its first loss for thirty years. It tries to get its money back from non-paying countries by renegotiating payments over a longer period at the PARIS CLUB.

Table 17 *ECGD insured exports as a percentage of total UK exports*

	UK exports	Exports made under contracts insured by ECGD	Percentage
1974	16309	5519	34
1975	19607	6902	36
1976	25277	9583	38
1977	31990	11253	35
1978	35380	13033	37
1979	40637	12654	31
1980	47339	14776	31
1981	50991	14337	28
1982	55538	15869	29
1983	50378	15194	30

Export Development Corporation. The EDC is Canada's EXPORT CREDIT insurance agency. It provides loans as well as insurance and GUARANTEES.

Export–Import Bank. Japan's state-owned export finance agency. Like the USA's EXIMBANK (but unlike its European counterparts), it also acts as a bank. And it administers some of Japan's aid programme. Japanese EXPORT CREDIT insurance and GUARANTEES are handled by the Export Insurance Division (EID) of MITI (the Ministry of International Trade and Industry). About 45 per cent of Japanese exports are covered by the EID.

Extended fund facility. A special fund of the INTERNATIONAL MONETARY FUND (IMF), available to help members who need to make structural adjustments to their economies. MEDIUM-TERM loan facilities are granted to qualifying countries. The country draws down the loan in TRANCHES, each tranche depending on the achievement of certain economic targets agreed in advance with the IMF.

At the end of January 1984 nine countries had extended fund-facility arrangements in place with the IMF. The total amount involved, in SPECIAL DRAWING RIGHTS (SDR), was SDR20.2 billion with the biggest amounts pledged to India (SDR5 billion), Brazil (SDR4.2 billion), Mexico (SDR3.4 billion) and Peru (SDR650 million).

Extraordinary general meeting (EGM). A special meeting of a company's shareholders called, in addition to the regular (compulsory) annual general meeting, to discuss something out of the ordinary.

F

Face value. The value on the face of a financial ASSET. A £1,000 TREASURY BILL has a face value of £1,000. But unless it MATURES today it is most unlikely that anybody will pay exactly £1,000 for it. They should pay more if INTEREST RATES are lower now than they were when the bill was issued.

Factoring. Getting someone else to collect your debts. A company will sell its RECEIVABLES to a factor (often the subsidiary of a bank) at a DISCOUNT. The factor then sets out to collect the money owed. His profit comes from collecting more than the discounted price he has paid for the debts.

The benefit to the company who employs the factor comes from the improvement in its CASH FLOW that results from receiving earlier repayment.

Fannie Mae. The name given to the Federal National Mortgage Association (FNMA), a semi-public body that bundles together MORTGAGES of American THRIFTS, GUARANTEES them and then issues SECURITIES backed by them. The enthusiasm of American investors for these securities over the past few years has been one of the most remarkable things seen in the USA's CAPITAL MARKETS. In 1983 $85 billion worth of mortgage-backed securities were issued: in 1973 scarcely $3 billion.

Fed funds rate. The RATE at which banks in America will lend to each other their surplus RESERVES – i.e. the extra non-INTEREST-bearing deposits that they hold with the FEDERAL RESERVE BOARD over and above what they need to meet their RESERVE ASSET RATIOS. These funds are prostitute money: held for just one night. The Fed can affect the Fed funds rate by adjusting the amount (i.e. the supply) of reserves that are in the banking system.

Federal Deposit Insurance Corporation (FDIC). The USA's DEPOSIT PROTECTION FUND. The FDIC insures all deposits up to $100,000 with banks that take out insurance cover with it. Some bright money BROKERS parcel out big deposits so that no one bank holds more than $100,000. The whole deposit is then fully insured.

Federal Home Loan Bank Board (FHLBB). The regulatory

authority that looks after most of the USA's SAVINGS AND LOAN ASSOCIATIONS. As these are allowed to become like banks, the FHLBB begins to overlap with the supervisory functions of bank regulators like the FEDERAL RESERVE BOARD and the COMPTROLLER OF THE CURRENCY.

Federal Open Market Committee. The supreme American monetary policy-setting committee. It meets about ten times a year in Washington, DC, to decide on policy guidelines; on it sit the seven governors of the FEDERAL RESERVE BOARD, the president of the Federal Reserve Bank of New York and the presidents of four other regional reserve banks.

Federal Reserve Board. The Federal Reserve System (known as the Fed) is CENTRAL BANK of the United States and thus the most powerful financial institution in the world. The Fed works through twelve regional federal reserve banks scattered throughout the United States. Each has nine directors who serve a three-year term. At the pinnacle of the system is the Federal Reserve Board, a board of seven governors based in Washington, DC. The chairman of that board is the 6 foot 5-inch, cigar-smoking PAUL VOLCKER.

The Fed carries out the usual monetary and foreign exchange responsibilities of a central bank. In addition, it is the supervisor of American bank holding companies. In practice, it keeps an eye on all American banks, for whom it is the ultimate LENDER OF LAST RESORT.

Fedwire. An automated information and money transfer system in the United States linking up its various federal RESERVE BANKS, the Treasury and a few member banks. Fedwire does three things:
- It transfers reserve ACCOUNT balances from one member to another.
- It gives instructions about the transfer of government SECURITIES.
- It transmits administrative and research information among its members.

Fiduciary deposits. A Swiss speciality in which a bank takes deposits and lends them on entirely at the depositor's own risk. The advantage for the bank is that the deposits remain off its balance sheet while it still makes a TURN on the transaction. The advantage for the depositor is a higher INTEREST RATE and the veil of Swiss SECRECY. Most FIDUCIARY DEPOSITS are simply passed on to other banks to become straightforward inter-bank Euro-currencies.

At the end of 1983 Swiss banks' fiduciary deposits amounted to SwFr 183 billion: 90 per cent of them came from abroad and SwFr 180 billion of them went back abroad.

Finance for Industry (FFI). Britain's LONG-TERM credit bank which recently changed its name to 3I in a blaze of trendy advertising. 3I is owned by a group of British banks and (its biggest single shareholder) the BANK OF ENGLAND. Its original purpose was to fill the gap in long-term finance for small and medium-sized companies. It now provides long-term finance for big companies as well. Small firms are served by its subsidiary ICFC.

FFI has recently branched out into some of the more fashionable forms of corporate finance. ICFC is a big arranger of MANAGEMENT BUY-OUTS, while another subsidiary, TDC, is big in VENTURE CAPITAL. It brought its first successful venture (the Scottish company Rodime) to the New York stockmarket in 1983, thereby making itself a tidy sum.

Finance house. Specialist companies in Britain (often subsidiaries of banks) which take in money from the MONEY MARKETS and lend it to individuals and companies for anything from one to five years to enable them to buy things like cars, fridges, plant and machinery. Finance companies also do a lot of LEASING.

In 1983 British finance houses lent £8.1 billion to industry and individuals, an all-time high. By the end of the year their total loans outstanding came to £14.5 billion, almost two and a half times what they had been five years earlier. For an individual, the trouble with borrowing from a finance house is that it is very much more expensive than borrowing from a bank. Make it your last port of call.

Table 18 *Finance Houses – outstanding credit*

To:	Consumers	Business	Leasing	Total
1979	1.94	2.38	1.67	5.99
1980	2.51	2.67	2.99	8.17
1981	3.01	2.95	4.16	10.12
1982	3.60	3.48	5.06	12.14
1983	4.70	4.12	5.53	14.35

New business 1983, by sector

Consumer	(£ m)	(%)	Business/Leasing	(£ m)	(%)
Used cars	867	22.8	Cars	1318	30.7
Personal lending,			Plant, equipment &		
Credit cards etc	815	21.4	oil	1068	24.9
New cars	730	19.2	Commercial vehicles	626	14.6
Home improvements	507	13.3	Computers & office	427	9.9
Domestic/Clothing	505	13.3	Farm equipment	182	4.2
Motor cycles	76	2.0	Aircraft & ships	66	1.5
Other	304	8.0	Other	610	14.2

Source: Finance Houses Association (of its members only)

Financial centre. Any place in which, for historical or tax reasons, more than an average amount of financial business (not just banking) is transacted. Centres can range from the big and indisputable, like London, to the small and ambitious like JERSEY or MACAU. See Table 19 p. 74.

Financial supermarket. Once upon a time it was thought safe to allow each financial institution to carry out only one type of financial service. So insurance companies sold insurance, banks gave loans and STOCKBROKERS sold shares. Now DEREGULATION has decreed that any financial institution can provide almost any financial service. So banks can sell shares and insurance companies can buy banks. These new financial conglomerates (like Shearson/AMERICAN EXPRESS in America and CHARTERHOUSE J. ROTHSCHILD/Allied Hambro in Britain) are colloquially referred to as financial supermarkets.

Table 19 *International banking by centre*

	End September 1983 $ b	End December 1973 $ b
Britain	662	95
United States	384	27
Japan	215	28
France	175	31
Bahamas	131	6
Singapore	112	6
Luxembourg & Belgium	{104 / 81	26
Swiss fiduciary accounts	84	12
Holland	66	10
Switzerland	69	18
W. Germany	63	15
Canada	66	13
Bahrain	58	—
Cayman Islands	46	n.a.
Hong Kong	64	n.a.
Italy	40	26
Panama	41	3

Note: All foreign currency lending plus domestic currency lending to non residents.
Source: Bank of England.

Financial system. The complete set of financial intermediaries involved in passing money and credit around a country's economy.

First Chicago. The fortunes of First Chicago, America's ninth biggest COMMERCIAL BANK, have been diametrically opposed to those of its close Chicago neighbour, CONTINENTAL ILLINOIS. When First Chicago's fortunes were low at the end of the 1970s, Continental Illinois was riding the crest of a short-lived wave. Tighter controls and a new chairman, Barry Sullivan, pinched from New York's CHASE MANHATTAN, have turned First Chicago round. Its increase in profits in 1983 (by 34 per cent to $183 million) was one of the biggest of any big American bank.

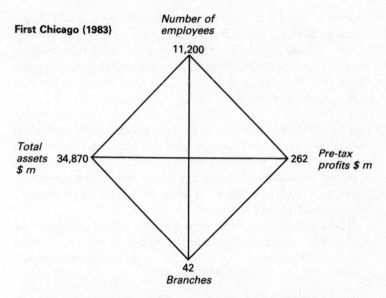

First Chicago (1983)

Number of employees
11,200

Total assets $ m   34,870

Pre-tax profits $ m   262

42
Branches

First National Bank of Boston. The USA's seventeenth biggest bank and one of three with claims to be the oldest in the country. First National Bank of Boston opened for business in July 1784, the same year as the Bank of New York. The First Pennsylvania Bank sometimes claims to be older but its advertisements have described it as 'banking since 1792'. And then only just. In 1980 it was saved from collapse by a $1.5 billion package from a group of other, healthier banks.

Fix. To manipulate a price. Usually considered to be nasty except when it is the fixing of the London GOLD price twice a day (at 10.30 a.m. and about 3 p.m.) by five big gold dealers, N. M. ROTHSCHILD, Mocatta & Goldsmid, Johnson Matthey, Samuel Montagu and Sharps, Pixley.

Fixed charge. SECURITY given by a borrower to a lender in the form of a claim on specific ASSETS of the borrower should he fail to repay. (See FLOATING CHARGE, where the claim is non-specific and against any of the borrower's assets.)

Fixed rate of INTEREST or of exchange; one that does not change over time. When one country sets its currency at an unchangeable RATE against another currency (say the pound was always equal to $2.40), it has a fixed rate of exchange. Most exchange rates are now FLOATING RATES. But countries whose trade is mostly denominated in dollars, fix their exchange rates against the dollar. In spite of that, their currencies float against every other currency, as does the dollar.

Fleming, Robert. No FINANCIAL SUPERMARKET this. A British MERCHANT BANK that has decided to specialize rather than generalize, Robert Fleming is the world's biggest dealer in Japanese CONVERTIBLE BONDS and one of the mightiest INVESTMENT MANAGERS in London. It owns 57.7 per cent of Britain's biggest UNIT TRUST group, Save & Prosper.

The original Robert Fleming was a jute trader in Dundee in the 1860s. His descendants include the author of the James Bond books, Ian Fleming, and his younger brother Richard, who was chairman of the bank from 1966 to 1974.

Flight capital. The money that rushes out of countries (and usually into Switzerland or the United States) when political or economic uncertainty make the maintenance of its value at home seem unlikely. Latin America's foreign debt problems in the early 1980s were exacerbated by the huge sums of money that its residents sent abroad as soon as trouble loomed. On one estimate over $60 billion fled Latin America between 1979 and 1982. When Mexico could no longer service its debts of $80 billion, Mexicans held at least $10 billion abroad in the form of bank deposits, and possibly as much as $20 billion worth of property, mostly condominiums in Florida.

Float. Two meanings:
• Money that arises in the ACCOUNTS of banks from double-counting CHEQUES that are in the process of being cleared. A pays B by cheque. When B puts the cheque into his bank it is credited to his account immediately. But for two or three days, until the cheque has been cleared (i.e. debited from A's account), there are two bank deposits for only one piece of money – in both A's and B's accounts. The double-counting is called the float and has to be excluded from statistics that aggregate all banks' deposits.
• See FLOATING RATE.

Floating charge. SECURITY given by a borrower to a lender that floats over all his ASSETS – i.e. if the borrower fails to repay the loan, the lender can lay claim to any of his assets, including stocks, RECEIVABLES, etc. Contrasts with a FIXED CHARGE.

Floating rate . . . of INTEREST or of exchange; one that changes frequently. A floating RATE of exchange between currencies is one that is determined (more or less) according to the laws of supply and demand. In practice, no exchange rate floats with total freedom. CENTRAL BANKS intervene to soften market forces, or governments manipulate their internal economies to give their currencies a boost.

Floating rate note (FRN). A BOND with a COUPON whose RATE varies in line with a market INTEREST rate. FRNs have become extremely popular in the EUROBOND market, where in 1983 they accounted for over 40 per cent of dollar-denominated Eurobond issues. FRNs appeal to borrowers at a time when they expect interest rates to fall and do not want to be locked into paying the FIXED RATES on traditional bonds.

In 1983 one bank, Crédit Suisse–First Boston, totally dominated the market for new issues of EURODOLLAR FRNs. It was lead manager of the first ISSUE to top $1 billion (for Sweden) and organized all four issues in the year of over $500 million.

Table 20 *Floating rate notes, 1983*

Lead managers	Total value $ b	Number of issue
Crédit Suisse – First Boston	4.69	23
Merrill Lynch	1.38	9
Banque Nationale de Paris	0.91	6
S. G. Warburg	0.57	7
Citicorp	0.56	4
Morgan Guaranty	0.56	9
Lloyds	0.51	4
Société Générale	0.48	5
Bank of America	0.30	5
Crédit Lyonnais	0.26	7

Source: Euromoney.

Fob (free on board). Used to indicate that a price quoted to an importer does not include the cost of insurance and shipping. To be contrasted with CIF.

Footsie. The affectionate name for the FT–SE 100 stock index, introduced on 1 January 1984 by the *Financial Times* and the London STOCK EXCHANGE. The index started life at a level of 1,000.

Footsie is a computerized index of 100 big British companies designed to fill the gap between the FT ordinary share index, which contains a mere thirty companies, and the FT all-share index, which contains hundreds and is calculated infrequently.

In May 1984 the first stock index OPTIONS and FUTURES to be traded in London were contracts based on Footsie.

Foreign bank. Any bank operating in a country other than the one in which it is registered. Foreign banks are generally welcomed

Table 21 *Foreign banks in London – April 1984*

Home country	Number
United States	126
Japan	58
Canada	25
Switzerland	22
Australia	21
France	21
Italy	21
Spain	17
West Germany	16
Brazil	12
India	10
Korea	10
Other European	73
Middle Eastern	35
Other Asian	31
Consortia	26
Other	41
Total	565

Source: Euromoney.

by FINANCIAL CENTRES, where they stick to foreign business (as in London, SINGAPORE, the BAHAMAS, etc.). They are not so welcome when they try to muscle into their host countries' domestic markets.

Foreign bond. BONDS denominated in a currency foreign to the domestic currency of the issuer and sold in the domestic market of the currency in which the bond is denominated – e.g. a Swiss franc bond issued by a Japanese company and sold in Switzerland. The line between foreign bonds and EUROBONDS is sometimes a fine one.

Foreign Credit Insurance Corporation (FCIC). A private American company owned by about fifty US insurance companies. Its main business is providing insurance against the commercial risk that a foreign importer will not pay an American exporter.

FCIC also acts as an agent for EXIMBANK in insuring against the political risks of exporting – for example, the risk that an importer will not be able to pay because his country has just had a military coup and all foreign debt repayments have been halted.

Forward cover. A way of guarding against unpredictable losses on payments due in the future. If a British company expects to receive $1 million in three months' time for some exports, it can make sure of how many pounds it is going to get by selling the $1 million forward in the currency FUTURES market. It then gets £x now for the promise to deliver $1 million in three months' time.

This method of forward cover eliminates the risk that a decline in the value of the dollar will wipe out the company's profit before it ever sees a payment. It also eliminates the chance that a decline in the value of sterling will make the value of the $1 million higher in three months' time than it is now. The more volatile an exchange RATE, the wiser it is for a company not in the business of dealing in currencies to take out forward cover.

Franklin National Bank. A big American bank that went bust in 1974. It was used by its biggest shareholder, MICHELE SINDONA, a

Sicilian who subsequently languished in a New York jail, to channel funds illegally around the world. After its collapse its remains were taken over by European American, a CONSORTIUM of seven big European banks. In the second quarter of 1984 trouble returned to the bank. European American reported a loss of $138 million, one of the biggest quarterly losses ever recorded by an American bank.

Freddie Mac. The name given to the Federal Home Loan Mortgage Corporation, an American semi-public body like FANNIE MAE that bundles together other people's MORTGAGES, GUARANTEES them and issues SECURITIES backed by them.

Free banking. There is no such thing as a free lunch, and there is no such thing as free banking. The expression is used to refer to a form of charging for CURRENT ACCOUNTS in Britain that imposes no charge for payments made from an account that is kept in credit.

Most British banks make no charge for payments if a minimum balance is kept in an account. One of the smaller London clearing banks, Williams & Glyn's, is the only one to offer 'free banking'. It has been an extremely successful marketing tool, increasing the bank's current accounts at an annual rate of about 20 per cent. The bank does not disclose whether it runs these accounts at a profit.

Friendly societies. See BUILDING SOCIETIES.

Frozen balance. Not an Eskimo's weighing scales but a bank ACCOUNT that has been made inaccessible for some reason (e.g. the government of the account holder is at war with the country in which the account is held).

Fungible. The quality of those things (like money) of which one individual specimen is indistinguishable from any other – i.e. if you are owed £1, it does not matter which particular pound note you are given even if it is frayed at the edges. Anything to be used as money (be it cowrie shells, beads or GOLD pieces) must be fungible.

Futures. Contracts to buy something in the future at a price agreed in advance. First developed in agricultural commodity markets, like those for potatoes and pork bellies, futures have now spread into financial and foreign exchange markets, EURODOLLAR deposits, government BONDS and stock indices.

Most innovative new contracts come out of Chicago and New York, but non–American FINANCIAL CENTRES like London, HONG-KONG, SINGAPORE and Sydney are setting up financial futures markets, often vying with each other to be the first to introduce new contracts. The LONDON INTERNATIONAL FINANCIAL FUTURES EXCHANGE opened in the old Royal Exchange building in the CITY of London in 1982.

G

Garnishee order. An order from a court forbidding a bank to release money that it holds in the ACCOUNT of Fred Bloggs for as long as Fred Bloggs owes money to Joe Soap. Joe Soap obtains the garnishee order and the bank is the garnishee. A few days after the order is given, the court has to decide whether Fred Bloggs's account should be used to settle Joe Soap's debts.

Gearing. The ratio between the amount of a company's CAPITAL that is in the form of debt and the amount that is in the form of EQUITY. Gearing can also refer to other relationships between parts of a company's capital – e.g. that between ordinary shares and PREFERENCE SHARES. The expression 'income gearing' refers to the proportion of a company's profits used to pay INTEREST.

Gentleman's agreement. All bankers, of course, are gentlemen, so whenever they have an agreement among themselves it is a gentleman's agreement. More strictly, a gentleman's agreement is an agreement which has no written proof of its existence. Bankers are fond of them because their favourite motto is 'My word is my bond', of which a cynic once said, 'If a man tells you that his word is his bond, take his bond.'

Giannini, A. P. The founder of the BANK OF AMERICA; a man who had all the elements of the American dream. The son of Italian immigrants, he made a small fortune trading on the San Francisco waterfront. He then made an even bigger fortune starting his own bank, the Bank of Italy, in 1904 to help what he saw as the badly-done-by small consumer. The Bank of Italy became known as the 'little fellow's bank', took over the Bank of America and became the biggest bank in the world just before A. P. Giannini died in 1949.

Gilt-edged. The quality ascribed to British government BONDS, known in consequence as 'gilts'. They are (supposedly) edged with gilt because of the low risk of DEFAULT – i.e. the assumption that the British government will honour them for ever and a day.

Ginnie Mae. The Government National Mortgage Association, a semi-public American institution that pools MORTGAGES issued by THRIFTS, insures them and then issues SECURITIES backed by them. American investors have taken to these securities in the past few years as if they were hot dogs. So popular have they been, they are now being specially packaged for European investors – as are their close cousins; FANNIE MAES and FREDDIE MACS.

Giro. A payment system organized by a group of banks or a postal authority which allows customers of one bank to make payments to customers in any other without the use of CASH or CHEQUES. The customer fills in an instruction form which is passed through a central CLEARING SYSTEM organized by the group.

Glass–Steagall Act. American legislation of 1934 put forward by Senator Carter Glass and Representative Henry Steagall. It stops COMMERCIAL BANKS (like CITIBANK and BANK OF AMERICA) from doing any UNDERWRITING or dealing in SECURITIES. Securities business is left as the exclusive preserve of INVESTMENT BANKS like MERRILL LYNCH and SALOMON BROTHERS.

This strict dividing line was erected in the wake of financial scandals in the 1920s and 1930s, when banks used depositors' money to support the price of securities they were underwriting, sometimes with disastrous consequences. Nowadays the dividing line is looking very frayed. The commercial BANK OF AMERICA has bought the big DISCOUNT BROKER Charles Schwab, which does no underwriting but is a big buyer and seller of securities.

Going concern. A concept dear to the hearts of accountants, it and the TRUE AND FAIR concept being the twin pillars of their profession. 'Going concern' refers to the implicit assumption in the accounts of companies that they will continue in existence in the foreseeable future. The assumption makes a difference. The value that you put on a pile of half-finished goods is very much higher if you assume that they are going to be finished and sold than if you assume that they will have to be flogged off as a half-finished job lot by a BANKRUPT company.

Gold. The precious metal that individuals most like to hoard when they feel uncertain about the value of money. CENTRAL BANKS like to hoard it too as part of their country's RESERVES. The world's biggest store of gold is held 80 feet below street level in the bedrock of Manhattan. The New York Federal Reserve Bank keeps gold there (its own and other people's) worth about $150 billion, almost a quarter of all the world's known gold.

Gold card. Up-market plastic cards issued by the TRAVEL AND ENTERTAINMENT CARD companies like AMERICAN EXPRESS and by credit card companies like BARCLAYCARD. 'Gold Card' was American Express's brand name but has become the generic name for super-plastic designed for rich, high-spending, far-travelling customers. For them the basic cards offer neither enough credit nor enough prestige.

Gold cards are given to those above a certain income level and usually provide OVERDRAFT facilities on favourable terms, reinforcing the well-known banking principle that the more you've got, the more you can get.

Gold clause. A clause in a loan agreement that fixes the borrower's repayment at an amount that is equal to the weight of gold that the original loan would have bought. Complicated? Not really. Suppose someone borrowed $100,000 when gold was $100 an ounce. If at repayment time gold cost $200 an ounce, then the borrower would have to repay $200,000 – i.e. the amount that would allow the lender to purchase the same weight of gold. When inflation is high and real INTEREST RATES are negative, gold clauses provide lenders with an incentive to part with their money in the expectation that their return will take care, at least, of inflation.

Goldman, Sachs. The American INVESTMENT BANK founded by Marcus Goldman in 1869. Mr Goldman started his business career selling buttons in New Jersey. His son-in-law, Samuel Sachs, joined the firm in 1882.

Goldman Sachs is now the biggest independent, privately owned investment bank in America. It also has an enviable reputation as one of the best. Its success in corporate finance has counteracted the bad times it (and all American investment banks) had in 1984 in their straight brokerage business.

Goodison, Sir Nicholas. Chairman of the London STOCK EXCHANGE and the man at the centre of the storm as British STOCKBROKERS move to DUAL CAPACITY, negotiate their COMMISSIONS and welcome outsiders (even foreigners) into their tight little club. See p. 86.

Government broker. The senior partner from the STOCKBROKING firm of MULLENS charged, since 1786, with the special job of handling the sale of new British government debt. The present government broker is Nigel Althaus. Because of its special position, Mullens is one broker that will not be allowed to be taken over by any old FINANCIAL SUPERMARKET.

Governor of the Bank of England. The boss man in the CITY of London. The Bank's first governor was Sir John Houblon (1632–1712), on whose house and garden the Bank stands today. Holders of the title since the First World War have been:

Sir Nicholas Goodison

1913–18 Mr Walter Cunliffe
1918–20 Sir Brien Cokayne
1920–44 Lord Norman
1944–49 Lord Catto
1949–61 Lord Cobbold
1961–66 The Earl of Cromer
1966–73 Lord O'Brien
1973–83 Lord Richardson
1983–   Mr ROBIN LEIGH-PEMBERTON

Gower, Jim. The septuagenarian professor of economics at Britain's Southampton University seconded to the Department of Trade and Industry to find a better way to protect investors from the wilder excesses of the CITY of London. His recommendations were published early in 1984 and included proposals for a new framework for policing the City. Anybody offering investment services would have to be a member of a self-regulatory agency or registered with the Department. The Gower Report will eventually give birth to new investor protection legislation.

Gower Report. See GOWER, JIM.

Grace period. The time between the granting of a loan (or, in the case of many developing countries recently, the RESCHEDULING of a loan) and the first repayment of the PRINCIPAL amount of the loan.

Grays Building Society. A small British BUILDING SOCIETY which went bust in 1978. It subsequently turned out that for decades its autocratic chairman had been funnelling away depositors' money for his own use. The chairman, Harold Jaggard, committed suicide a few weeks before the scandal came to light.

The Grays affair first awoke the authorities to the fact that the supervision of small building societies left something to be desired. How many others were being run, like the Grays, as personal financial fiefdoms? Since then the supervision of societies has been tightened up – a bit.

Greenback. Slang for the world's favourite currency, the dollar.

Gross. The opposite of NET; a total given before any deductions have been made. For example, gross income is income before taxation, gross domestic product (the most popular measure of economic activity in a country) is the value of its output of goods and services before any deduction is made for the depreciation of the country's capital investment or for taxation.

Guarantee. An undertaking by a third party to be responsible for a loan from a bank should the borrower go BANKRUPT or do a bunk. To be legally binding, a guarantee must be made in writing.

H

Halifax. Britain's biggest BUILDING SOCIETY and, it claims, the biggest building society in the world. At the end of January 1984 its total ASSETS were £16.8 billion, making it one-quarter the size of Britain's biggest bank, BARCLAYS. Almost 7 million people had savings with the Halifax; and over 1 million had MORTGAGE loans from it. In 1983 it gave 187,000 new mortgages and became the first building society to install through-the-wall AUTOMATED TELLER MACHINES. These brought it into closer competition with the banks.

In spite of its size and sophistication, the Halifax still has its headquarters in the old Yorkshire woollen town whose name it bears.

Hambros. An old British MERCHANT BANK founded in the nineteenth century by the Scandinavian Carl Joachim Hambro, several of whose scions still work for the bank today. It soon sat (along with N. M. ROTHSCHILD and BARING BROTHERS) at the pinnacle of the London banking establishment.

The bank got into deep water in the 1970s when it financed much of the oil-tanker empire of the Norwegian magnate Hilmar Reksten. When Reksten went belly-up, Hambros was left holding seven very large tankers in a glutted market.

It was kept out of serious trouble by the best investment it ever made – its large stake in Hambro Life, an insurance-based financial services group, which it sold to CHARTERHOUSE J. ROTHSCHILD for £126 million in 1984. Like many other merchant banks, Hambros has now put a toe into STOCKBROKING via a link-up with the broker Strauss Turnbull.

Hard currency. A currency that people want to hold because they do not expect its value to be eroded by inflation, the opposite of soft currency whose value melts away even as you hold it. Traditional hard currencies are the dollar, the Deutschmark, the yen, the Swiss franc and (on and off) sterling.

Hedge. Behaviour which reduces the risk of loss from future price movements. Thus in Britain in the 1970s, when inflation was rampant, people bought property because they thought that it would keep its value even if NOTES and COIN did not. Their property was a hedge against future inflation.

Hedging can also be applied in financial markets. A British company that is expecting to receive dollars in three months' time can sell them now and get a known amount of sterling for its dollars. It has then hedged against the dollar's devaluation in the intervening three months.

Hermes. West Germany's EXPORT CREDIT insurance agency. Hermes (full name Hermes Kreditversicherungs) is privately owned but grants GUARANTEES on behalf of the federal government. It provides insurance for both export credits and domestic credits. About 8 per cent of all West Germany's exports are covered by Hermes.

Herstatt. A West German bank that collapsed in 1974 from losses in the foreign exchange market. It was the first significant disaster in the then burgeoning EUROMARKET and became an object lesson thereafter in what dangers had to be avoided and how. Ten years later, in February 1984, the chairman of the bank, the 70-year-old Ivan Herstatt, was convicted of fraudulently concealing foreign exchange losses of DM100 million in the bank's 1973 accounts. He managed to avoid trial for many years through illness and was eventually convicted four months before West Germany's ten-year statute of limitations would have brought any proceedings to an end.

Hidden reserves. What some banks are allowed to hide from the eyes of the reader of their balance sheets. This they do by valuing ASSETS in their books at less than their real value, thus leaving their liabilities understated (i.e. their reserves at less than what they should be).

The practice of squirrelling away hidden reserves is slowly disappearing. The big British CLEARING BANKS voluntarily gave up their legal right to hold certain hidden reserves in the late 1960s. But other British financial institutions like DISCOUNT HOUSES and MERCHANT BANKS still cling to the privilege.

In other countries hidden reserves are commonplace. The HONGKONG AND SHANGHAI BANK is reputed to have some of the largest hidden reserves in the world. Swiss banks too are notorious for their Alpine reserves. The third biggest, CREDIT SUISSE, managed to cover a SwFr 1.7 billion loss from its Chiasso branch in 1977 with hardly a franc showing in its accounts – i.e. almost entirely out of hidden reserves.

High net worth individual. A new buzz phrase in banking – the sort of customer every bank wants: he earns a lot, travels a lot, spends a lot and needs a lot of financial advice and a lot of loans (which he is sure to repay). A phrase in search of an acronym.

Hire purchase. A combination of hiring and purchasing. The purchaser hires a consumer product (like a car) while he or she makes a series of regular payments. When the payments are finished the product automatically becomes the property of the hirer. Specialized financial institutions have grown up to provide the loan part of a hire-purchase agreement. Their RATES are usually much higher than those of an ordinary bank's personal loans.

Historic cost accounting. The original set of rules by which companies drew up their accounts and in which most of their ASSETS were valued at whichever was the lower – their cost or their current value. The set of rules has been thoroughly disturbed by recent enthusiasm for different forms of INFLATION ACCOUNTING. These try to take into account the fact that inflation rapidly increases the cost of replacing assets – something a company must do now and again if it is to maintain its value (i.e. its capacity to continue to produce the same stream of income).

Hoare, C., & Company. One of the longest surviving British PRIVATE BANKS. As recently as 1955 the six partners of the bank were all Hoares, descendants of the founder Richard Hoare (1648–1718). Now the bank has two branches, is still privately owned and has eleven Mr Hoares working for it.

Home banking. Banking done at home by means of a television screen, a little black box and telephone lines. It has enormous potential but at the moment is limited to a few small experiments (e.g. those of the Nottingham Building Society in Britain and of Chemical Bank in New York).

Surveys in America say that of all the services to become available on home computers, banking will be the most popular.

With the craze for the personal/home computers just beginning, banks are starting to take home banking seriously. It took twenty years for plastic cards to take off and ten for AUTOMATED TELLER MACHINES. Will home banking take five?

Hongkong. The British colony and volatile Far Eastern FINANCIAL CENTRE, much of which reverts to China in 1997. It has come up against increasing competition from SINGAPORE for the crown of top financial centre in the region. In spite of uncertainty about what the Chinese might do with it after 1997, Hongkong has retained the edge in terms both of the number of foreign banks that maintain their regional headquarters there and of innovative financial markets.

Hongkong and Shanghai Banking Corporation. Known simply in Hongkong as 'the Bank', this mammoth institution (the eighteenth biggest bank in the world in terms of shareholders' funds) dominates the financial affairs of the British colony. It acts like a CENTRAL BANK, holds about 60 per cent of the colony's deposits and owns a big chunk of the airline Cathay Pacific and of a newspaper, the *South China Morning Post*. The chairman, Michael Sandberg, also sits on the Colony's governing legislative council.

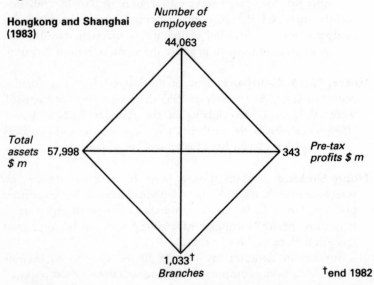

Hongkong and Shanghai (1983)

Number of employees 44,063

Total assets $ m 57,998

Pre-tax profits $ m 343

1,033[†] Branches

[†]end 1982

Powerful at home, the bank has proved unpopular abroad. Its takeover of New York's Marine Midland Bank was fiercely opposed by the New York authorities. Only by turning Marine Midland into a national rather than a STATE-CHARTERED BANK did the takeover succeed. Similarly, in Britain when the bank tried to take over the ROYAL BANK OF SCOTLAND it was fiercely (and successfuly) opposed by the then GOVERNOR of the BANK OF ENGLAND, Gordon Richardson. Secretive and paternalistic, it is difficult to guess where the bank could now turn to escape from its overcrowded home base.

Hot money. CAPITAL that flows to wherever it finds the highest return. Since it has no long-term allegiance to any one investment, its flow back and forth across exchanges (as relative real INTEREST RATES change) can cause wild fluctuations in exchange rates – fluctuations that disturb CENTRAL BANKERS who like to see rates move in an orderly fashion.

Hot money also refers specifically to the types of note found in Italian suitcases crossing into Switzerland.

I

Indexation. Maintaining the value of a financial ASSET in line with inflation. So an indexed savings deposit of £100 would be worth £105 after a year in which the inflation rate was 5 per cent.

Inflation accounting. The philosopher's stone sought by businessmen, accountants and professors that will turn base HISTORIC COST ACCOUNTING into the golden truth – the measure of a company's real performance at a time of inflation. So far the search has proved elusive. Britain and the USA have occasionally thought they have discovered the next best thing. Never mind: a lot of people are thoroughly enjoying the search. Let them carry on. Just don't try to understand them.

Insolvency. Strictly, the condition of a company whose liabilities (what it owes) exceed its assets (what it owns and what it is owed). Not all insolvent companies end up in the corporate graveyard. Understanding creditors may help them to work themselves out of insolvency. More often than not, insolvent companies are "wound up" with their creditors getting whatever they can from the forced sale of the company's assets.

Instalment credit. A loan that is repaid over a period in regular, equal instalments. FINANCE HOUSES specialize in providing instalment credit – usually used to buy things like cars, fridges and freezers. It is also, more rarely, used to finance trade.

Institute of Bankers. Housed in famous LOMBARD STREET, in the heart of the CITY of London, the Institute of Bankers is one of the world's oldest professional associations. Its aims are to educate and inform its thousands of members, most of them involved in banking business around the world.

Inter-American Development Bank. The biggest regional development bank (see ASIAN DEVELOPMENT BANK and AFRICAN DEVELOPMENT BANK). Set up in 1959 and based in Washington, DC, it raises money in the CAPITAL MARKETS of rich ORGANIZATION FOR ECONOMIC CO-OPERATION AND DEVELOPMENT countries and lends it to not-so-rich countries in Latin America. The bank's highest authority is its board of governors, on which each of the forty-three member countries is represented. The board meets once a year – in 1984, in the Uruguayan seaside resort of Punta del Este.

In 1983 the bank made seventy-four loans worth $3 billion. Over its twenty-five-year history about one-quarter of the bank's lending has gone to energy projects, another quarter to agriculture and fisheries, and about 15 per cent to transport and communications. The biggest beneficiaries have been Brazil, Mexico, Argentina and Colombia, in that order.

Inter-bank market. The market in which banks deal with each other – a very important part of any efficient banking system. Some banks get more deposits than requests for loans, and vice versa. The inter-bank market smooths out these imbalances by providing a way for a bank with too many deposits to pass them on to a bank with too many loan requests.

In London there are different inter-bank markets for different currencies and for deposits with different MATURITIES. Of these, the EURODOLLAR inter-bank market is particularly important, and LIBOR (the London inter-bank offered rate) is a key dollar rate for all the world's international borrowing and lending.

Inter-Bank Research Organization. A research body set up by all the big British CLEARING BANKS in 1968 to study subjects of common interest. These range from political issues, like the impact of the EUROPEAN ECONOMIC COMMUNITY or of tax proposals in the budget, to more practical questions of how best to automate CLEARING SYSTEMS or to harmonize the numbered coding of CHEQUES.

Interest. That which is charged to the customers of a bank for the privilege of borrowing other people's money. Or (the other side of the same coin) that which is paid to the customers of a bank for the honour of lending their money to somebody else.

International Bank of Reconstruction and Development (IBRD).
See WORLD BANK.

International Banking Act. A piece of American legislation passed in 1978. Its main aim was to allow foreign banks to operate inside America on the same terms as American banks. That had advantages and disadvantages: it allowed foreign banks to do things that they had not been allowed to do before (like opening up EDGE ACT subsidiaries), but it also stopped them doing things (like branching across state boundaries) that were not permitted to domestic American banks.

International banking facilities (IBFs). New York's attempt to bring some of the EUROMARKET back home. IBFs were introduced in December 1981. They are separate units of banks in the United States (mostly in New York) that are allowed to lend and take deposits outside America free of reserve requirements and any INTEREST RATE ceilings imposed on the banks' domestic business. In their first month almost $65 billion flooded into the IBFs.

International Development Association (IDA). Set up in 1960 as an arm of the WORLD BANK, IDA is a twentieth-century Robin Hood, internationalized and institutionalized. It takes money from the world's richest countries to lend it LONG-TERM (for up to fifty years, INTEREST-free and with a ten-year GRACE PERIOD) to the very poorest. By the middle of 1983 IDA had lent $30 billion for projects in seventy-nine countries in Asia, Africa, the Middle East and Latin America.

International Finance Corporation (IFC). Set up in 1956 as an arm of the WORLD BANK, the IFC invests in the private sector in developing countries. It grants private companies loans and (sometimes) takes EQUITY stakes in them.

International Monetary Fund (IMF). The nearest thing to a world CENTRAL BANK. Set up by the high-powered conference at Bretton Woods which redesigned the world monetary order in 1944. Its purpose was to oversee the system of fixed exchange rates which then prevailed, but it has become more famous in recent years as fire-fighter for the world's debt problems. The IMF leads the way for COMMERCIAL BANKS and other developing country creditors by getting troubled countries to agree to impose stiff economic programmes in return for its loans. Once such programmes are in place, bankers *et al.* are happy to RESCHEDULE their loans and, sometimes, to lend more.

There are over 140 members of the IMF. Most come from the non-communist world, although Hungary and Poland have recently become members, and Yugoslavia has been a member for longer. Each country pays a membership fee (its quota) which is related to the size of its economy. Members can then borrow up to 25 per cent of their quotas at will; any more and they have to accept certain conditions from the IMF as to their economic performance. The managing director of the IMF (currently Jacques de Larosière) is usually a European, the deputy managing director (Richard Erb) an American.

The Fund has its headquarters in Washington, DC, where a lot of clever people from around the world (each according to his quota) worry about monetary and economic problems. Just pray that they are clever enough.

Investment bank. In its most general sense, a bank that provides LONG-TERM loans and/or EQUITY CAPITAL to industry (e.g. as in the EUROPEAN INVESTMENT BANK). More specifically, it refers to American institutions like MERRILL LYNCH, GOLDMAN SACHS and SALOMON BROTHERS that UNDERWRITE and deal in SECURITIES. Investment banks also provide a number of other advisory services to companies (e.g. on takeovers). They combine the functions of British MERCHANT BANKS, STOCKBROKERS and stock JOBBERS.

America's GLASS–STEAGALL ACT divides investment banking from COMMERCIAL BANKING so that the same institution cannot do both. But, led by Merrill Lynch, the investment banks have begun to offer a number of services (like the CASH MANAGEMENT ACCOUNT) that look remarkably like deposit-taking services – the bread and butter of commercial banks. Shed no tears: the commercial banks are fighting back and will soon be able to do investment banking. Many of them already provide 'no-frills' DISCOUNT BROKERAGE services.

Investment manager. A professional investor who manages trust funds, pension funds, etc., within the general guidelines laid down by the trust itself. That leaves him a lot of discretion, and these shadowy, unknown people are among the most influential in any financial market.

Investment trust. A company set up for the purpose of holding the shares of other companies. Investment trusts are useful to small shareholders who do not have enough money to invest in a wide-ranging PORTFOLIO. By buying the shares of an investment trust, the shareholder can effectively buy a small part of all the shares that the trust holds in its own portfolio. Investment trusts sell, on average, at a 30 per cent DISCOUNT to their net ASSET values – i.e. their shares are worth 30 per cent less than the MARKET VALUE of the shares they hold.

Invisible trade. Trade that never sees the inside of a container but earns foreign exchange nevertheless. Services like banking, insurance and tourism make up the biggest part of invisible trade. Some countries (like Britain) have a big surplus on their invisible trade account because they have a lot of people (like bankers) who spend their time coming in and out of Heathrow Airport. Others (like West Germany) have a big deficit because a large proportion of Germans like to take their holiday money abroad.

Table 22 *The world's invisible trade*
(excluding government transactions)

Top earners 1982	Net $ b	Gross $ b
United States	47.0	118.4
Britain	10.8	46.3
France	7.3	63.7
Switzerland[1]	6.8	14.2
Singapore[1]	5.7	10.6
Bottom earners		
Canada	−13.8	11.4
West Germany	−16.3	38.9
Brazil[1]	−16.6	3.2
Japan	−16.9	33.0
Saudi Arabia	−20.0	5.3

Note:
[1] including government transactions.
Source: British Invisible Exports Council.

Issue. The process of selling new securities (BONDS or shares); in Britain, the speciality of ISSUING HOUSES. New issues can be made in several ways: through an "offer for sale" in which the issuing house buys the securities from the company and then sells them to the public; through a direct sale by the company itself; or through a private placement with a limited number of investors.

Issue price. The price at which shares or BONDS are first issued to the public. This may not be the same as the nominal price which is on the face of the SECURITIES (i.e. their FACE VALUE).

Issuing house. A number of posh London MERCHANT BANKS that do the cream of the business of sponsoring and UNDERWRITING new capital ISSUES by British companies. In 1945 they formed themselves into a CITY club and called it the Issuing Houses Association. Its membership overlaps somewhat with the even more exclusive ACCEPTING HOUSES COMMITTEE.

J

Jersey. One of a group of British islands called the Channel Islands. Although located in the English Channel, they are nearer to France than to England. They have a certain amount of fiscal and legal independence from the mainland. This has allowed Jersey to become an OFFSHORE BANKING centre especially useful for British expatriates' savings.

Jobber. The wholesaler of SECURITIES on the London STOCK EXCHANGE. Strictly separated from the retailer, the STOCKBROKER. Because of Britain's system of SINGLE CAPACITY, jobbers cannot be brokers and vice versa. When the London Stock Exchange moves from fixed to negotiated COMMISSIONS on securities transactions (scheduled to happen before the end of 1986) the distinction between jobbers and brokers should disappear.

In anticipation of that day, other financial institutions have begun to buy stakes of up to 29.9 per cent (the maximum allowed for the moment) in British firms of jobbers.

Jobber's turn. Where the JOBBER makes his profit – the difference between the price he pays for the SECURITIES that he buys and the price he gets when he sells them.

Junk bond. BOND issues by companies whose RATINGS are below what would normally be acceptable to the market. In 1983 $7.5 billion worth of such (theoretically unissuable) bonds were issued.

K

Kaffirs. The shares of South African gold-mining companies.

Kleinwort Benson. Britain's biggest MERCHANT BANK with assets of £4.2 billion. It was founded in the 1830s by Alexander Kleinwort, a German merchant in the Cuban sugar trade. It still has a trading arm which now specializes in Eastern European business. It owns the precious metals BROKER Sharps, Pixley (see FIX), one of the thirty-seven PRIMARY DEALERS in government SECURITIES in the USA, and 5 per cent of the British STOCKBROKER Grieveson Grant, which it intends to take over fully when it is allowed to.

Krugerrand. A South African gold COIN that contains exactly 1 ounce of pure gold. Krugerrands containing ½ ounce, ¼ ounce and ¹⁄₁₀ ounce of gold have also been issued. Their neat simplicity and a forceful marketing campaign have made Krugerrands very popular with investors who (for reasons like tax avoidance) often prefer to hold gold as coins rather than as ingots. In 1970 only 211,000 ounces of Krugerrands were sold around the world. At their most popular (in 1978) 6 million ounces were sold. In 1983 the figure was 3.5 million ounces.

L

Landesbank. Regional banks in West Germany that act as mini-CENTRAL BANKS for the host of powerful local SAVINGS BANKS. In the 1970s the *Landesbanken* grew out of this limited function and began to look more like UNIVERSAL BANKS, branching out into international lending and other COMMERCIAL BANKING specialities. The biggest – Westdeutsche, Hessische and Bayerische Landesbanken – became household names in the EUROMARKET.

Laundering. Pejorative word with connotations similar to 'whitewash'. Laundering is the process of passing money through a very secret sieve (like a Swiss bank) or through a series of extraordinarily complicated transactions that disguise its true origin or purpose from (for example) tax inspectors, the Fraud Squad or both.

Lead manager. The bank which leads the organization of a SYNDICATED LOAN or of a jointly UNDERWRITTEN ISSUE of SECURITIES. The lead manager does most of the donkey work in the negotiations with the borrower and guarantees to take up the largest part of any issue that is left unsold. For that, of course, it gets the biggest fee and top billing on the TOMBSTONE.

Leasing. The hiring of CAPITAL GOODS or equipment to avoid the all-at-once cost of buying them. Leasing is popular in places like Britain, where it can be used to take advantage of generous tax allowances. Manufacturing companies do not pay much tax because of the capital allowances they set off against their taxable income. If they want to buy capital goods, they can be better off leasing them from companies like banks, which do pay tax.

The bank buys the capital goods (like plant or planes), sets the capital cost off against its taxable income and then leases the goods to the manufacturer. One study reckoned that in Britain 80 per cent of the tax benefit to the leasing bank was passed on to the lessee in the form of lower charges.

Governments usually like leasing because they want to encourage capital investment. However, the 1984 Budget in Britain set about cutting back capital allowances. The benefits of leasing will become correspondingly less.

Legal tender. A method of payment that, by law, must be

accepted as settlement of a debt (i.e. pound notes or dollar bills but not conch shells or luncheon vouchers).

Leigh-Pemberton, Robin. Christened Robert, known as (and signs his name as) Robin. The new GOVERNOR OF THE BANK OF ENGLAND (appointed in 1983), formerly chairman of the biggest bank in Britain, NATIONAL WESTMINSTER, and a keen cricketer. His appointment aroused controversy because he was seen as a political appointee, his Thatcherite sympathies being no secret. But, as the London *Times* put it: 'Though he is Thatcher's man, he does not seem to be making the Bank her creature.'

Lender of last resort. The ultimate responsibility of a CENTRAL BANK is to act as lender of last resort – typically, to provide the banks under its charge with enough money to stop a RUN on the bank. All banks are illiquid (the average MATURITY of their loans exceeds the average maturity of their deposits), so should all depositors demand their money back simultaneously, there is no way the banks could meet the demand. They could not call in their loans fast enough.

Walter Bagehot's classic exposition of the role of a central bank as lender of last resort argues that the only way to stop a run on a bank at no cost is to pump limitless amounts of money into it. Depositors then know they are safe and, when their fears have subsided, the central bank can pull back the money it pumped out.

Less developed country (LDC). Not quite as nice as 'developing country' as a description of most places which are not members

Table 23 *Largest developing country debtors[1]*

	$ b		$ b
Brazil	93	Indonesia	25
Mexico	89	Philippines	25
Argentina	44	Yugoslavia	20
Korea	40	Chile	18
Venezuela	34	Turkey	17

Note:
[1] total external debt, end 1983.
Source: Amex Bank.

of the ORGANIZATION FOR ECONOMIC CO-OPERATION AND DEVELOP-MENT (OECD). Since the condition of an LDC is relative (less developed than what?), it is not a precisely defined term. Is South Africa (not a member of the OECD) an LDC? Are Brazil and South Korea? Once an LDC, always an LDC?

A rough rule of thumb for bankers is that LDCs are those countries (mostly in the southern hemisphere) that borrowed more money in the 1970s than they could cope with in the 1980s.

Letter of credit. An arrangement with a bank to make money available abroad. The customer's ACCOUNT is debited with an amount, and his bank then instructs its CORRESPONDENT BANK, in whatever place the customer wants the money, to make it available on demand. The bank will send its correspondent a sample of the customer's signature.

Leutwiler, Fritz. At only 60 years old, Europe's grand old man of CENTRAL BANKING. The unstuffy president of the Swiss National Bank and chairman of the BANK FOR INTERNATIONAL SETTLEMENTS (BIS). A steadfast fighter against inflation in the 1970s and a firm handler of Switzerland's redoubtable COMMERCIAL BANKERS. Under his chairmanship the BIS made its first BRIDGING LOANS to hard-pressed debtor countries. In 1984 he announced that he would retire from the Swiss National Bank and the BIS at the end of the year. See p. 105.

Leverage. The indebtedness of a company compared to its EQUITY capital. A highly leveraged company is one with a high proportion of bank loans to equity (see GEARING).

Leveraged buy-out. An increasingly popular way (particularly in the United States) of buying companies. The buyer takes a large EQUITY stake without putting up much money. Most of the purchase price comes from bank loans secured on the ASSETS of the company being bought. Some wise bankers (like WALTER WRISTON) think that leveraged buy-outs will be the cause of the next American banking crisis. Older American bankers were brought up to see red lights flashing when a company's debt rose above 50 per cent of its equity.

Fritz Leutwiler

Table 24 *Leveraged buy-outs*
(largest deals 1979–83)

Company purchased	Price $ m	P/E	Premium over market value (%)
1983 Metromedia	1468	44.5	140.0
1983 Wometco Enterprises	810	29.6	16.6
1981 Twentieth-Century Fox	683	12.3	11.6
1983 Dr Pepper	512	n.a.	37.5
1981 Reliance Group	483	10.0	16.7
1979 Congoleum	447	9.8	43.4
1983 Amstar	429	20.1	47.5
1982 Signode	426	13.9	32.5
1981 Norris	420	16.4	47.2
1981 Fred Meyer	398	17.9	41.9

Source: W. T. Grimm & Co.

Liability. Anything owing to somebody else. Most companies' and most individuals' liabilities are the ASSETS of banks (i.e. loans). Banks' liabilities are the deposits they take from their customers and the BONDS and BILLS they ISSUE. If a company's assets do not exceed its liabilities it is insolvent. The amount by which the one exceeds the other is the company's "net worth" (or shareholders' funds).

Liability management. The business of managing a bank's LIABILITIES (essentially its deposits) so that their RISK, MATURITY and LIQUIDITY are matched with the shifting demand for loans (the bank's ASSETS) in a way that optimizes its return – i.e. offers it the best reward for the risk it is taking (see ASSET MANAGEMENT).

LIBOR (London inter-bank offered rate). The queen bee INTEREST RATE in the EUROMARKET; the rate which top-class banks in London will pay each other for EURODOLLARS.

Most Euromarket lending is pegged to the three- or six-month LIBOR. The excess of the lending rate over LIBOR is the bank's MARGIN (i.e. its profit) on the loan.

LIBOR is a FLOATING RATE. It is changing all the time. So rates charged to Euromarket borrowers also change during the period of the loan. One reason why Latin America had difficulty repaying its loans to Western banks was that it badly underestimated the ability of dollar rates (including LIBOR) to climb out of single figures.

Some borrowers prefer to peg their rates to America's own domestic PRIME RATE as an alternative to LIBOR. They might have been better off borrowing Swiss francs if they could have got them.

Licensed deposit-taking institution. The second rank of banking recognition given in Britain under the BANKING ACT of 1979. In the first rank are RECOGNIZED BANKS, which carry out a full range of banking activities. Licensed deposit-takers are limited essentially to the taking of deposits and the granting of straightforward loans. There are two possible reasons for having a licence instead of becoming a recognized bank:
- The institution does not want to offer a full range of services.
- The BANK OF ENGLAND does not want it to offer a full range of services.

Licensed deposit-takers may not call themselves banks unless they are registered abroad and 'Bank' is part of their registered name. (For example, the Bank of Credit and Commerce International, a LUXEMBOURG-based institution which has many branches in Britain, is a licensed deposit-taker.) There are about 310 deposit-takers licensed by the Bank of England.

Lien. The obtaining of the rights to property (in the widest sense of the word – i.e. not just bricks and mortar) until a debt from the owner of the property is repaid. After a lien has been obtained, the debtor remains the legal owner of the property, although he loses his right to sell it.

Lifeboat. A scheme launched by the BANK OF ENGLAND in 1974 to rescue some of the large number of secondary banks in distress (see SECONDARY BANKING CRISIS). Big and wise British banks put up some £1.2 billion to support small and foolish banks that had lent too exuberantly to the property market before it collapsed in 1973. At the time there were rumours that not even the big banks had all been wise.

The logic for the rescue rested on the belief that banks are special. Their business is based on the psychology of confidence. If enough banks close down and destroy that confidence, then all banks become threatened. The argument against launching mutual support systems like the lifeboat is that they encourage others to undertake lucrative but foolish landing, knowing that if they get into the dirt deeply enough, they will be rescued for the good of us all.

Limited liability. What the wheel is to the car, limited liability is to capitalism. It confines the losses that the owners of a company can incur to a maximum of the amount of CAPITAL that they have put into the company.

Liquidation. A company's final burial. Although most liquidations in Britain are done by accountants or solicitors, they can in practice be done by anybody. Recent scandals have turned the spotlight on cowboy liquidators who end up getting more out of terminally ill companies than do its creditors. Legislation will soon ensure that all liquidators are registered with the government.

The liquidator's main job is to get the maximum amount possible for the company's creditors from whatever ASSETS are left. This may be as little as one penny in the pound. Clever liquidators can, however, sometimes recover much more. The liquidator of Laker Airways, for example, decided to use what money was remaining to creditors to sue the big transatlantic airlines and to accuse them of causing Laker's downfall by agreeing among themselves to cut their fares by however much it took to put Laker out of business.

Liquidity. Two meanings:
- Short-term ASSETS like cash and easily sellable SECURITIES (as in LIQUIDITY RATIO). From this can be deducted SHORT-TERM borrowing to get the net liquidity of a business.
- The MATURITY of a financial market – i.e. the ability of investors in it to find buyers for their investments quickly and at the going market price.

Liquidity ratio. The PRUDENTIAL RATIO that is used to ensure that a bank can meet most unexpected demands for CASH from its depositors. Liquidity ratios have traditionally concentrated on comparing a bank's deposits with its 'liquid' ASSETS ('liquid' being defined in many different ways). In 1982 the BANK OF ENGLAND came up with a new form of liquidity ratio based on comparing a ladder of assets and LIABILITIES. Each rung on the ladders represented a different (narrow) range of MATURITIES.

Listing. The addition of a company's CAPITAL to the list of shares and debt instruments that are traded on a particular STOCK EXCHANGE. The process of obtaining a listing can be expensive – as a rule, the higher the status of the exchange, the more it costs.

Lloyd's. The London insurance market that first began in Edward Lloyd's CITY coffee house in the eighteenth century. It is now run through a complicated arrangement of 'names', who get together in syndicates and pledge their (considerable) worldly wealth to UNDERWRITE almost any sort of risk you like to name.

The market has recently been tainted by scandals in which income due to the names has been siphoned into OFFSHORE BANKING centres by the managers of the insurance syndicates. The names were making so much anyway, they hardly noticed.

Note the apostrophe in the spelling of Lloyd's – the only way to distinguish it from the big British bank LLOYDS.

Lloyds Bank. The smallest of the big four London CLEARING BANKS. Lloyds has a strong RETAIL BANKING business and more AUTOMATED TELLER MACHINES than any other clearing bank. It also has a strong business in Latin America through its old subsidiary, the Bank of London and South America (once known as BOLSA).

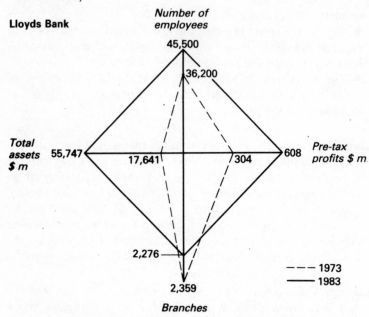

Its Latin American links have brought it much unwelcome attention. It was the only British bank with a branch network in Argentina at the time of the Falkland Islands squabble, and it has lent a lot of money to hard-pressed debtors south of the Rio Grande.

Loan guarantee scheme. A scheme introduced in 1981 in which the British government guarantees (for a 3% premium) up to 80% of loans made by banks to small expanding businesses. By the end of 1983, loans worth £440 million had been made under the scheme to more than 13,500 small companies – of which about 1500 had subsequently gone bust.

Loan stock. That part of a company's CAPITAL issued in the form of INTEREST-bearing LONG-TERM loans or BONDS. (See DEBENTURE.)

Lombard rate. The key INTEREST RATE in West Germany, Lombard rate is the rate at which the BUNDESBANK lends to COMMERCIAL BANKS when loans are secured by top-grade ASSETS like TREASURY BILLS and BILLS OF EXCHANGE.

Lombard Street. A famous narrow street in the CITY of London that owes its name to the Italian bankers from Lombardy who set up shop there in the fifteenth century. Many of Britain's best-known banks have their head offices on Lombard Street, including the Italianate marbled and fountained home of BARCLAYS BANK at number 54.

London International Financial Futures Exchange (LIFFE). Housed in the old Royal Exchange building right across the street from the BANK OF ENGLAND. LIFFE first breathed in 1982 and now trades in about seven different financial FUTURES contracts, two or three of which are highly successful (the three-month EURODOLLAR deposit and the GILTS future, for example), the others less so.

London Metal Exchange. Housed in Plantation House in the CITY of London, where seven different metals (copper, lead, zinc, tin, silver, aluminium and nickel) are traded by thirteen member dealers who scream at each other across the trading RING.

Long-term. A long-term loan is one whose MATURITY exceeds five years. Bankers rarely contemplate lending for longer than fifteen years.

Longs. British government SECURITIES (GILTS) with a MATURITY of more than fifteen years.

Luxembourg. The smallest member of the EUROPEAN ECONOMIC COMMUNITY but with pretensions to being its biggest FINANCIAL CENTRE. It has attracted a large number of FOREIGN BANKS (particularly from West Germany and Sweden) which find it more accommodating to their international business than a base back home.

Luxembourg is also a major EUROBOND centre, as investors find its anonymity convenient. It suffered a big blow to its prestige when BANCO AMBROSIANO collapsed, taking BAH, its Luxembourg subsidiary, with it. Foreign banks had lent BAH over $600 million and were left to whistle for their money for a very long time.

M

Macau. A Portuguese colony off the Chinese coast, not too far from HONGKONG. Sometimes it looks as if it would like to be a FINANCIAL CENTRE, but it has two handicaps: it lives in the shadow of Hongkong, and it has no decent banking legislation. Fourteen FOREIGN BANKS have an office in the colony, including three from Portugal. Citicorp is the only big American bank there.

McFadden Act. One of the most important pieces of American banking legislation, the McFadden Act was passed in 1927. It placed NATIONALLY CHARTERED BANKS on the same footing as STATE-CHARTERED BANKS as far as branching was concerned. In effect, that meant that no American bank could have branches outside its home state. Although the legislation is still in place, its effect has been diluted. Banks have found loopholes that have allowed them to cross many state boundaries. There will, for example, soon be few states where CITICORP does not have a banking business.

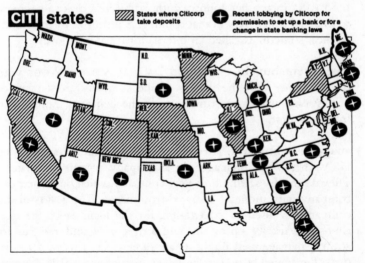

CITI states — States where Citicorp take deposits — Recent lobbying by Citicorp for permission to set up a bank or for a change in state banking laws

Spare a thought for poor Mr Pepper. The McFadden Act was originally named the Pepper–McFadden Act after the two Congressmen who sponsored it (like the GLASS–STEAGALL ACT). For some unexplained reason, history has obliterated Mr Pepper from the record books.

Macmillan gap. The big discovery of the Macmillan Committee, which reported on the financing of British industry in 1931: that small and medium-sized firms had great difficulty raising Britain's CAPITAL MARKETS as they then existed. Since the report several institutions, have been set up to fill the gap – with limited success. More useful has been the UNLISTED SECURITIES MARKET, set up in 1980 as the London STOCK EXCHANGE's junior market for smaller firms.

Mag stripe. The magnetic stripe on the back of a plastic CREDIT CARD that allows electronic machinery to check that the card belongs to the person who has just punched a PERSONAL IDENTIFICATION NUMBER into the machine. In a remarkable feat of standardization, the mag stripe is the same size, in the same place and contains a similar sort of coding wherever the plastic card on which it sits is issued.

Mail transfer. A letter from a customer's bank to its CORRESPON-DENT BANK in another country authorizing it to make a payment to a named beneficiary in that country. A primitive form of trade finance, sometimes called an international payment order.

Management buy-in. Similar to a MANAGEMENT BUY-OUT with the difference that the buyers of the company are a team of professional managers from outside the company rather than from within it.

Management buy-out. A recent phenomenon in Britain and the USA whereby the managers of a company become its owners. They do this by setting up a new company which buys their old company with money borrowed from banks. The ASSETS of the company are used as COLLATERAL for the loan. Since the deal almost invariably raises the company's debt and reduces its EQUITY, management buy-outs are often called LEVERAGED BUY-OUTS. Leveraged buy-outs, however, are not necessarily done by the management.

One of the earliest and most successful examples in Britain was the buy-out of the National Freight Corporation.

Manufacturers Hanover. New York's third and the USA's

fourth biggest bank, Manny Hanny (as it is known) has become one of the world's biggest international lenders with special expertise in Eastern Europe and an awful lot of loans in Latin America. It was one of the first and most successful of the American COMMERCIAL BANKS to open up an INVESTMENT BANKING business in London. There it was allowed to operate in the EUROMARKET in a way that it is still forbidden by the GLASS-STEAGALL ACT to do in the United States.

Margin. The deposit that an investor puts down to buy SECURITIES. The rest is often lent to him by his BROKER, who is confident in the knowledge that the investor can always sell the security to repay the loan. The margin payment (the deposit) is designed to be at least as big as the maximum fluctuation possible in the MARKET VALUE of the security. If the price starts to fall drama-tically, the broker may make an extra 'margin call' on the investor – i.e. ask him to increase his deposit.

Market capitalization. The value of a company as measured by its stockmarket price – i.e. the number of shares multiplied by the MARKET VALUE of a share. For all sorts of reasons the market capitalization of a company may differ enormously from its book value – i.e. what its accounts say is its net worth (its ASSETS minus its LIABILITIES).

Market value. What someone is actually prepared to pay now for something. Loans have a market value because banks can usually find someone (probably another bank) to buy them at a price. Even Latin American loans change hands these days – though the DISCOUNT on their FACE VALUE is kept a closely guarded secret.

MasterCard. The other amorphous international payment system like VISA, MasterCard is a co-operative set up by a group of banks from around the world to make it easier for their customers to pay for goods and services. In Britain the most visible sign of the MasterCard's emblem of two Californian oranges is on the front of the ACCESS card. Access is a member of the MasterCard system.

Matching. The process by which a bank chooses ASSETS (i.e. loans) which match its LIABILITIES (i.e. deposits) in terms of currency, MATURITY or geographical region (see RISK). No bank matches the two sides of its balance sheet perfectly. If it did, it would not make much profit. The bank's skill resides in getting the right degree of mismatching to maximize profit.

Maturity. The life expectancy of a loan. Original maturity is the length of time from the beginning of a loan to the date of the last repayment. Residual maturity is the time from today until the final repayment.

Maturity transformation. What banks do to earn their living: borrow short and lend long – i.e. transform the short MATURITIES of most of their deposits into the longer maturities of their loans. Institutions like Britain's BUILDING SOCIETIES perform the most dramatic maturity transformation, taking in deposits which can be withdrawn almost on demand and lending them out in loans which are not fully repaid for up to twenty years.

Medium-term. Medium-term bank loans are those with an original MATURITY of between one and five years – i.e. shorter than LONG-TERM and longer than SHORT-TERM.

Mercantile House. One of the new breed of FINANCIAL SUPER-MARKETS being raised in London. Started out as a money BROKER; now a broker of much else besides. Under the guidance of its chief executive, John Barkshire, Mercantile House has (within two years) gone into American brokerage (it bought Oppenheimer in 1982), British STOCKBROKING (it took 29.9 per cent of Laing & Cruickshank in 1984) and the DISCOUNT MARKET. In 1984 it bought not one but two DISCOUNT HOUSES (first Alexanders, then Jessel, Toynbee & Gillett) within four months of each other. Next stop Tokyo?

Merchant bank. Those British banks which concentrate on advising companies about raising new CAPITAL and about buying or selling other companies. They do a bit of straight lending too, but not much. Some of them also specialize in fund management, UNIT TRUSTS and/or insurance broking. The big CLEARING BANKS have only recently begun to build up their own merchant banking subsidiaries. The snobbiest merchant banks are all members of the ACCEPTING HOUSES COMMITTEE. Some of them are the offspring of the families that founded the banks in the eighteenth and nineteenth centuries as the financial arms of big 'merchant' trading houses.

Table 25   *British companies' financial advisers*

Merchant bank	No. of quoted company clients end 1983	end 1980
Hill Samuel	100	117
S. G. Warburg	100	100
N. M. Rothschild	86	54
Morgan Grenfell	85	64
Kleinwort Benson	85	86
Schroders	75	82
County Bank	67	65
Baring Brothers	57	53
Samuel Montagu	53	61
Barclays Merchant Bank	49	44

Source: Crawford's Directory of City Connections.

Table 26   *Advisers on mergers and acquisitions, 1983*

	Number	Value (£ b)
Morgan Grenfell	39	2.74
S. G. Warburg	21	1.45
Hill Samuel	22	1.37
Lazard Brothers	10	1.17
Kleinwort Benson	37	0.95
Schroders	7	0.80
Charterhouse Japhet	10	0.73
N. M. Rothschild	21	0.67
Samuel Montagu	34	0.60
Baring Brothers	21	0.52

Cont. overleaf

Table 26 *cont.*

Rights issues and flotations, 1983

| | Flotations | | Rights issues | |
	Number	Value (£m)	Number	Value (£m)
Schroders	26	1,589	8	161
Kleinwort Benson	9	926	12	301
Morgan Grenfell	12	884	21	664
Lazard Brothers	6	693	4	62
S. G. Warburg	7	482	4	63
County Bank	10	121	10	90
Samuel Montagu	11	103	5	229
Robert Fleming	6	102	6	69
Charterhouse Japhet	2	71	n.a.	n.a.
N. M. Rothschild	6	60	5	279
Hill Samuel	n.a.	n.a.	6	302

Source: Financial Times

Merrill Lynch. The biggest of the USA's SECURITIES firms –
known sometimes, unaffectionately, as the 'thundering herd'
because of an old advertisement which showed a number of bulls
with the caption 'Merrill Lynch is bullish on America.' Mr
Charles Merrill and Mr Edmund Lynch got together to start the
firm in 1914. They grew big by taking the stockmarket to
America's high streets.

The company, unlike many of its rivals, is publicly QUOTED. It has a branch network across the United States, through which it sells vast quantities of securities but which is also very expensive. Of all the USA's big brokers, it has moved farthest in eroding the barriers between banking and broking created by the GLASS–STEAGALL ACT. It invented the CASH MANAGEMENT ACCOUNT in 1977, which really set the broking cats among the banking pigeons. Invention, however, has not been the mother of profits: 1984 was one of Merrill Lynch's worst years ever.

Midland Bank. Britain's third biggest bank and the one most closely associated with financing Britain's mainstream industrial companies. Of all the British banks, Midland has the strongest presence in continental Europe, with big subsidiaries in France and West Germany. It also owns the well-known travel agent and TRAVELLER'S CHEQUE issuer, Thomas Cook.

Midland Bank was the first British CLEARING BANK to have a woman on its board, and could well soon be the first to have a foreigner. The blot on Midland's copybook is its huge American subsidiary, the Californian Crocker National Bank. It made a bundle of bad loans before Midland bought it – loans that only came to light later.

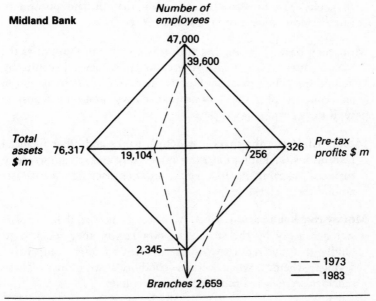

Midland Bank

Number of employees

47,000
39,600

Total assets $ m 76,317   19,104   256   326   Pre-tax profits $ m

2,345

Branches 2,659

--- 1973
— 1983

Minimum lending rate. This was the key INTEREST RATE in Britain between 1973 and 1981, the rate at which the BANK OF ENGLAND lent money to the DISCOUNT HOUSES. Minimum lending rate (known as MLR) succeeded BANK RATE and was replaced by nothing. Britain switched to a different system of monetary control that did not have a formal declared interest rate as its focus.

Mint. The place where metal is turned into COINS, usually under government guidance if not under direct government ownership. In the United States coins are minted in Philadelphia, Denver and San Francisco under the control of the US Treasury.

MITI. The short name for Japan's Ministry of International Trade and Industry, home of the shadowy bureaucrats who direct the Japanese economic miracle and much of the activity of its financial markets besides.

Mixed credits. Usually known by their French name, *crédits mixtes*, since the French are particularly fond of them. A mixture of aid and trade finance whereby exports to developing countries from developed ones are given every bit of financial assistance available. The CONSENSUS lays down that the aid portion of mixed credits must not be less than 20 per cent.

Monetary base. The smallest sum it is possible to think of as the MONEY SUPPLY, of which there are now several confusing definitions. The monetary base is the currency in circulation in an economy plus the COMMERCIAL BANKS' RESERVES deposited with the CENTRAL BANK.

Money market. The market in which banks and other financial institutions (including CENTRAL BANKS) buy and sell SHORT-TERM financial instruments like BILLS and CERTIFICATES OF DEPOSIT among themselves.

Money market account. When American banks had their deposits snitched away by the MONEY MARKET FUNDS, they moaned so loudly that the regulators allowed them to offer competitive savings schemes when certain conditions were met. These schemes were called money market accounts.

Money market fund. An American fund which invests in the MONEY MARKET. When American banks' ordinary customers were prevented from getting a decent RATE of return on their deposits by REGULATION Q, money market funds, by pooling together enough small deposits to gain access to the money market (where INTEREST rates were not controlled), were able to offer savers market-related rates of return. Of course, money flocked out of bank ACCOUNTS and into the money market funds.

Money shops. A fashionable phrase in Britain in the 1970s for a number of financial institutions that tried to compete with the big banks by opening branches that were supposed to be like shops. They could be booths on railway stations or offices where the tellers sat behind shop-like counters rather than bars. These money shops did not, however, take off in a big way. They are now about as rare as Victorian pillar boxes.

Money supply. The expression signifies different things to different people in different places. In Britain there are at least seven definitions of money supply (or the amount of money circulating in the economy). These are: MO (the very latest model), M1, M2, Sterling M3, M3, PSL1 and PSL2. Their relationship to each other can best be illustrated by a chart.

Monopolies and Mergers Commission. The independent body called upon by the British government to look into planned takeovers which might (or might not) create monopolies, and to see if they are in the 'public interest'. In practice, the Commission can be asked to investigate any bid which would result in merged ASSETS worth more than £30 million (raised from £15 million in August 1984) even if there is not the slightest hint of a monopoly. Bids which lead to merged assets worth less than £30 million can be referred to the Commission if they result in a market share of 25 per cent or more. Whatever decision the Commission reaches can always be overturned by the government.

The Commission is always in danger of becoming a scapegoat for the government in any bid it does not favour (such as the HONGKONG AND SHANGHAI BANKING CORPORATION's bid for the ROYAL BANK OF SCOTLAND in 1980). Its inexact criteria are a great

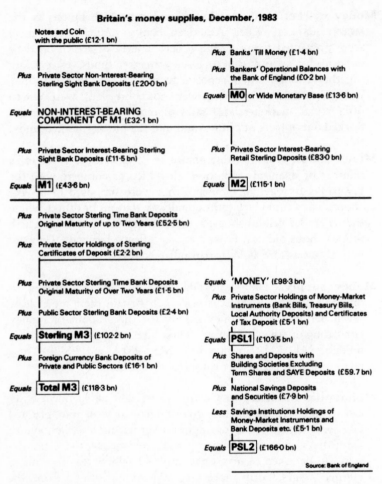

Britain's money supplies, December, 1983

Notes and Coin with the public (£12·1 bn)

Plus Banks' Till Money (£1·4 bn)

Plus Bankers' Operational Balances with the Bank of England (£0·2 bn)

Equals **M0** or Wide Monetary Base (£13·6 bn)

Plus Private Sector Non-Interest-Bearing Sterling Sight Bank Deposits (£20·0 bn)

Equals NON-INTEREST-BEARING COMPONENT OF M1 (£32·1 bn)

Plus Private Sector Interest-Bearing Sterling Sight Bank Deposits (£11·5 bn)

Plus Private Sector Interest-Bearing Retail Sterling Deposits (£83·0 bn)

Equals **M1** (£43·6 bn)

Equals **M2** (£115·1 bn)

Plus Private Sector Sterling Time Bank Deposits Original Maturity of up to Two Years (£52·5 bn)

Plus Private Sector Holdings of Sterling Certificates of Deposit (£2·2 bn)

Plus Private Sector Sterling Time Bank Deposits Original Maturity of Over Two Years (£1·5 bn)

Equals 'MONEY' (£98·3 bn)

Plus Private Sector Holdings of Money-Market Instruments (Bank Bills, Treasury Bills, Local Authority Deposits) and Certificates of Tax Deposit (£5·1 bn)

Plus Public Sector Sterling Bank Deposits (£2·4 bn)

Equals **Sterling M3** (£102·2 bn)

Equals **PSL1** (£103·5 bn)

Plus Foreign Currency Bank Deposits of Private and Public Sectors (£16·1 bn)

Plus Shares and Deposits with Building Societies Excluding Term Shares and SAYE Deposits (£59·7 bn)

Equals **Total M3** (£118·3 bn)

Plus National Savings Deposits and Securities (£7·9 bn)

Less Savings Institutions Holdings of Money-Market Instruments and Bank Deposits etc. (£5·1 bn)

Equals **PSL2** (£166·0 bn)

Source: Bank of England

nuisance to MERCHANT BANKS trying to advise their corporate clients about whether or not to go ahead with a bid.

Monte dei Paschi di Siena. The oldest bank (and the biggest mouthful) still recognizable in Europe as a bank today. In 1972 Monte dei Paschi di Siena celebrated its 500th anniversary. In the sixteenth century the Italians were bankers to Europe. They have left their mark in names like Britain's LOMBARD STREET, at the heart of London's banking district, and in West Germany's LOMBARD RATE.

Moratorium. A period, agreed between a borrower and a lender, in which repayments of PRINCIPAL are allowed to lapse. Common in troubled Latin America.

Banks do not like to give a moratorium on INTEREST payments because this does nasty things to their accounts. In practice, several Latin American countries got so far behind with repayments of both interest and principal in the early 1980s that they were implicitly granted a moratorium on interest as well as principal.

Morgan, John Pierpont. America's most famous nineteenth-century banker. Born with a big nose and a rich father, he made himself a legend by financing the construction of American railroads. He died in Rome in 1913. His family's name lives on in the American banks that grew out of his empire MORGAN STANLEY and MORGAN GUARANTY, and in the British MERCHANT BANK that his father established in London, MORGAN GRENFELL. Only since Morgan Guaranty sold its last 33.3 per cent stake in Morgan Grenfell in 1981 have the three banks been entirely separate from each other.

Morgan Grenfell. The British MERCHANT BANK set up by the father of J. P. MORGAN in the eighteenth century. It is, therefore, a sort of first cousin to the American banks MORGAN GUARANTY and MORGAN STANLEY. Morgan Grenfell has the best reputation in Britain for making or defending takeovers, a business in which reputations can quickly come and go. The bank is one of the few merchant banks that are still private companies. As the breakdown of the CITY of London's financial separations (see SINGLE CAPACITY) is likely to increase the need for capital, the bank is thinking about going PUBLIC with a stockmarket LISTING scheduled for 1985. Meanwhile it has bought 29.9 per cent of a stock JOBBER, Pinchin, Denny, and 19.9 per cent of a life assurance/UNIT TRUST group, Target.

Morgan Guaranty. The poshest COMMERCIAL BANK that the USA has got. Its headquarters have been on the same WALL STREET corner since 1873. It scorns the business of most ordinary mortals, demanding a large minimum deposit before it honours them with its services. It prefers to deal with governments and companies.

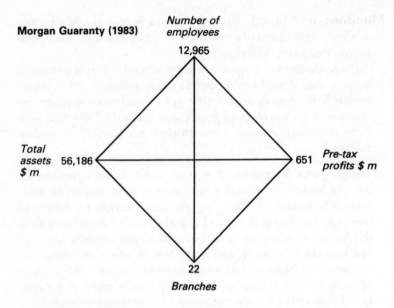

Morgan Guaranty (1983)

Number of employees

12,965

Total assets $ m   56,186

Pre-tax profits $ m   651

22

Branches

Morgan Guaranty is the commercial banking bit of the financial empire built up by the great American snob J. P. MORGAN. Its strength lies in its trust department, which manages about $30 billion worth of American fortunes – so much that it can sometimes dominate dealing on the mighty NEW YORK STOCK EXCHANGE in a particular share.

Morgan Stanley. The INVESTMENT BANKING arm of J. P. MORGAN'S banking empire. Morgan Stanley was split off in the 1930s when the GLASS–STEAGALL ACT decreed that investment banking be separated from COMMERCIAL BANKING. It is still one of the most prestigious WALL STREET investment banks and one of the few that has remained in private hands. Many speculate that with the coming of FINANCIAL SUPERMARKETS, it will be difficult for the likes of Morgan Stanley to remain privately owned and to continue to raise enough CAPITAL for the ever-increasing range of business open to them.

Mortgage. The transfer of an interest in property to someone else as SECURITY for a loan. The most common type of MORTGAGE is one for the purchase of a house in which the mortgage bank or

BUILDING SOCIETY holds the deeds of the property. A second mortgage is merely a second loan on the security of the same property. In Britain building societies are not allowed to give second mortgages. At the end of 1983 Britons had £90.8 billion worth of mortgages, 75 per cent of them (by value) from building societies.

Moussa, Pierre. The chairman of PARIBAS, the French MERCHANT BANK, immediately before it was nationalized in 1981. He resigned soon after but was pursued by the French government, outraged at his sale to foreigners of Paribas' big Swiss subsidiary just before nationalization. In 1984 he was finally acquitted of charges of breaking exchange controls.

Mullens. The CITY of London's oldest stockbroking firm, Mullens has supplied the GOVERNMENT BROKER since that office was first established in 1786. This places the firm in a unique relationship with the BANK OF ENGLAND and the financial markets.

Mutual savings banks. A group of American financial institutions found mostly in the East Coast states of New England. They are much like SAVINGS AND LOAN ASSOCIATIONS in that their staple

Table 27   *Ten largest American savings banks*

	Deposits at 31st December ($ b)		Home town
	1982	1983	
Philadelphia Saving Fund Society			
Goldome Bank for Savings	8.62	9.99	Philadelphia
Metropolitan Savings Bank	7.55	9.83	Buffalo
Dime Savings Bank of New York	5.30	7.08	Brooklyn
Anchor Savings Bank			
Bowery Savings Bank	5.55	6.13	Brooklyn
Dollar Dry Dock Savings Bank	2.42	5.19	Northport
Sears Savings	4.55	5.09	New York
Great American Federal Savings	2.48	4.73	Bronx
Bank	2.52	3.80	Los Angeles
Long Island Savings Bank			
	3.20	3.59	San Diego
	1.13	3.21	Syosset

Source: American Banker.

business is the provision of a safe home for savings. They differ in that they are, according to some definitions, banks and for many purposes (e.g. regulation) treated as such. They are all STATE-CHARTERED BANKS and some are insured by the FEDERAL DEPOSIT INSURANCE CORPORATION.

N

Napoleon. A French gold COIN with a FACE VALUE of 20 francs.

National Association of Securities Dealers' Automated Quotations (NASDAQ). The computerized system of dealing in shares in America. NASDAQ is an OVER-THE-COUNTER MARKET sponsored by the National Association of Securities Dealers.

Table 28 *Nasdaq – main shares traded, 1983*

Company	Market[1] capitalization ($m)†	Shares traded (m)
MCI Communications	3,374	330
Apple Computer	1,441	201
Glaxo Holdings	—	122†
Philips (NV)	—	107†
Intel Corporation	4,664	100
Tandon Corporation	1,003	95
Convergent Technologies	856	89
Seagate Technology	607	89
Tandem Computers	1,402	82
Fuji Photo Film	—	59†

Notes:
[1] 31/12/83.
† Traded in ADR form.
Source: Nasdaq.

National Savings. The British government's own personal savings schemes against which no financial institution can compete. The government sets a target each year that it wants National Savings to suck in, and then sets its rates to ensure that it reaches the target. The target for 1983/84 was £3 billion, duly achieved. The target for 1984/85 was the same. Banks and BUILDING SOCIETIES heaved a sigh of relief: that represented a drop in real terms and left more savings for them.

National Westminster Bank. The biggest COMMERCIAL BANK in Britain but not the biggest British bank. That honour belongs to BARCLAYS BANK by virtue of its bigger overseas business.

National Westminster (widely known as NatWest) is one of the biggest employers in Britain and one of the biggest bank employers in the world, with over 70,000 people on its payroll.

NatWest had a rough time in the 1970's property débâcle, but (perhaps as a result of being extra cautious thereafter) it is now one of the top banks in the world in terms of its American credit market ratings. It has had less trouble than its British rivals with its diversification into the USA, although its purchase there (the National Bank of North America, now renamed National Westminster, USA) is only just beginning to justify the high price paid for it.

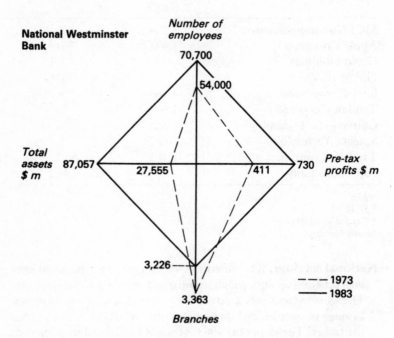

National Westminster Bank

Number of employees

Total assets $ m

Pre-tax profits $ m

Branches

- - - 1973
——— 1983

Nationalization. The buying and running of companies by the state. In many European countries some of the biggest COMMERCIAL BANKS are nationalized. In France the three biggest were nationalized before President Mitterrand decided (in 1981) to take over most of those that were not.

The French have a different attitude to banks from that of

Anglo-Saxon countries, believing that money is more like the air in which business operates (and therefore in the public domain) than something out of which private enterprise should itself make money.

Even in countries where the main commercial banks are not nationalized, a big chunk of the flow of private savings may still pass through government control via NATIONAL SAVINGS (as in Britain) or through banks that are owned by local authorities.

Nationally chartered bank. American banks can choose where they get their charter (i.e. permission) to operate as a bank. Either they can get it from their home state and become a STATE-CHARTERED BANK, or they can get it from the COMPTROLLER OF THE CURRENCY and become a nationally chartered bank. Which charter they have determines who is to be their chief regulator – one of the fifty state banking superintendents or the Comptroller.

Banks sometimes shift from a state to national charter if one authority is not allowing them to do something that they think the other will. Marine Midland Bank, America's fourteenth biggest, switched from being chartered in New York state to being nationally chartered when the New York state banking superintendent at the time, Muriel Siebert, would not allow the HONGKONG AND SHANGHAI BANKING CORPORATION to take it over. The ploy was successful. The Comptroller did allow the take-over to go ahead.

Narrow market. A market in which only a small supply is available of whatever it is that market sells – e.g. particular shares on the stockmarket, or a particular currency in the foreign exchange market.

Negotiable instrument. A financial instrument that can be handed from one owner to another without informing the issuer of the instrument – e.g. a bank NOTE, a bearer BOND, a CHEQUE, a CERTIFICATE OF DEPOSIT, etc.

Net. The opposite of GROSS; a loosely used word meaning what is left after certain deductions have been made. Confusion arises when you try to decide which deductions. Hence net profit is profit that is left after deducting from the gross profit the expenses incurred in running the business. Which expenses? Well, that depends.

Similar quandaries can surround net income (income after tax), NET WORTH (ASSETS minus LIABILITIES), net investment (investment less DEPRECIATION) and net CASH FLOW (a company's cash flow after DIVIDENDS have been paid out).

Net worth. The value of a company calculated by subtracting its outstanding LIABILITIES from the current value of its total ASSETS. If this is negative, the company is technically INSOLVENT. It may be possible for it to carry on trading if it has tolerant creditors. Many big companies have had a negative net worth for a while and yet have survived (e.g. many American SAVINGS AND LOAN ASSOCIATIONS).

New Cross Building Society. One of Britain's fastest growing BUILDING SOCIETIES in the late 1970s, it was closed by the societies' supervisor, the CHIEF REGISTRAR OF FRIENDLY SOCIETIES, at the end of 1983. The Registrar maintained that the society had broken statutory ratio requirements. In a key judgement a court of appeal upheld the Registrar's decision, saying, in effect, that even if the society had not broken any rules, it was within the Registrar's powers to close it.

None of the society's depositors lost any money. All its obligations were taken over by the much bigger Woolwich society.

New York Futures Exchange (NYFE). Pronounced 'knife', it rhymes with LIFFE (the London International Financial Futures Exchange). NYFE was set up in 1979 as a subsidiary of the NEW YORK STOCK EXCHANGE to provide eastern seaboard competition to Chicago's growing domination of FUTURES trading.

New York Stock Exchange (NYSE). The world's biggest and most prestigious stock exchange. The MARKET CAPITALIZATION of all the companies quoted on the NYSE is a staggering $1.5 trillion. Think of all the noughts: $1,500,000,000,000. The market capitalization of the biggest company on the NYSE (computer giant IBM) is alone worth more than $70 billion, more than the value of all shares traded on the Australian stock exchange, the sixth biggest in the world.

Table 29 *New York Stock Exchange: most traded shares, 1983*

Company	Market[1] Capitalization ($b)	Shares traded (m)
AT&T	57.4	389
IBM	74.0	223
Exxon	33.9	211
Chrysler	3.2	183
General Motors	23.4	152
Pan American	0.7	141
Merrill Lynch	2.6	141
Eastman Kodak	12.7	131
Citicorp	5.1	130
American Express	6.7	127

Notes:
[1] 31/12/83.
Source: NYSE.

The NYSE was first constituted under the Buttonwood Agreement of 17 May 1792, so called because it was signed under a buttonwood (sycamore) tree.

Newly industrialized countries (NICs). An expression devised to bridge the gap between the old industrialized countries of Europe and North America and the LESS DEVELOPED COUNTRIES of the Third World. Most NICs are in the Far East – places like South Korea, Taiwan and Singapore.

Night safe. A method pre-dating AUTOMATED TELLER MACHINES by which banks tried to extend their opening hours without actually staying open. Night safes are metal chutes, covered with retractable lids, that pass through the wall of a bank branch. Customers can take a wallet from the branch and a key to the chute. They can then open the chute any time in the night, put inside the wallet whatever it is they want to give to the bank for safekeeping, and throw it down the chute. Very useful for casinos, all-night garages, and other businesses that take a lot of CASH outside normal banking hours.

Nominee. Someone whose name is used in place of somebody else's. To ensure greater secrecy for a Swiss bank ACCOUNT, the beneficiary of the account might open it in the name of a nominee. The nominee would then pass on all the INTEREST to the true beneficiary, whose name need never be known to the bank.

An agreement among Swiss banks limits the scope for this. They have agreed that they will always try to find out who is the true beneficiary of an account before they allow it to be opened.

Nomura Securities. The biggest Japanese STOCKBROKER, Nomura has spread its wings around the world: 11 per cent of its pre-tax income now comes from its thirty overseas branches, the rest from its 106 domestic branches. Nomura's president, Setsuya Tabuchi, believes that the ratio will be 50:50 by the end of the 1980s. Nomura's name is now linked with that of MERRILL LYNCH as being the two companies most likely to dominate trading when fully international capital markets arrive.

The Japanese FINANCIAL SYSTEM was restructured along American lines after the Second World War. Japanese SECURITIES houses like Nomura are allowed to do more or less the same things at home as are their American counterparts in the United States. They cannot do COMMERCIAL BANKING but they combine the functions carried out in Britain by MERCHANT BANKS, stockbrokers and JOBBERS.

Non-performing loan. A concept in American bank accounting. Loans are considered to be non-performing when no INTEREST has been paid on them for at least ninety days. When they cross the critical ninety-day threshold (and become non-performing) the loans have to be reported as such in the banks' accounts. All the interest due (which the banks up until then have reported as having come in) has to be pruned out of their income for the period.

The best-known non-performing loans are those to Argentina. When they became more than ninety days overdue, they chopped an average of 3 per cent off big American banks' reported earnings.

Non-voting shares. Shares which give their owners no voting rights in companies' affairs. Such shares are frowned on in

Britain, but in countries like Canada they have been used by big companies to increase their CAPITAL without diluting control, the small number of voting shares remaining in the hands of a few people, often connected with a single family.

Nostro account. An expression used by someone at bank A when talking to someone at bank B to refer to bank A's account with bank B. Based on the Latin *noster*, meaning 'ours' – i.e. 'our account with you'. (See VOSTRO ACCOUNT.)

Note. Two meanings:
- Paper money – or maybe, in the near future, plastic money. There have been several experiments with plastic notes that have all the features of the paper kind – that is, they are secure, thin, malleable and easily countable. The Isle of Man, an offshore British island, has already issued very respectable plastic notes, but the Bank of England is opposed to churning them out on the mainland. Plastic notes are not as easily destructible as paper ones. (The Federal Reserve Bank of New York destroys more than $7 million of tatty dollar bills every day.)
- A type of debt SECURITY, as in FLOATING RATE NOTE and PROMISSORY NOTE.

Now (Negotiable Order of Withdrawal) account. An account that can be opened only by individuals (not corporations) at banks and THRIFTS in America. The account pays INTEREST and allows CHEQUE-like things called negotiable orders of withdrawal to be drawn on it. First introduced experimentally in Massachusetts in the early 1970s. NOW accounts only became legal nationwide in 1981. They have not grown as fast as interest-bearing checking accounts should – partly because the authorities have kept the maximum interest RATE they can offer relatively low.

Numbered account. A Swiss invention designed to give depositors the ultimate in secrecy. In fact it is far less secret than mythology would have it. The numbered ACCOUNT (Swiss-style) differs from an ordinary Swiss account only in the number of people within the bank who know the name of the account holder – limited to three or four senior executives. The rest of the staff know the account only by its number.

Other countries have tried to make numbered accounts more secret by ensuring that nobody at all knows the account holder's name. This has created problems when the account holder has died and his or her heirs have come along to try to lay claim to the monetary remains.

Numismatism. The study and collection of old COINS – a pastime that can be hazardous to the eyesight and harsh on the hands.

O

Odd Lot. A stockmarket transaction in a smaller number of shares than the usual minimum amount required for trading (often 100 shares).

Off-cover. When countries are not sufficiently creditworthy to pay for loans with which they have bought their imports, EXPORT CREDIT agencies, like Britain's EXPORT CREDITS GUARANTEE DEPARTMENT (ECGD) put them off-cover – i.e. they refuse to GUARANTEE bank loans for financing exports to those countries. That leaves three options:
- A bank takes the risk.
- The exporter himself takes the risk.
- The business is called off.

In mid-1984 only three countries (Argentina, Poland and Zambia) were completely off-cover with ECGD. When such countries pull up their financial socks, they come back 'on-cover'.

Official receiver. A civil servant who can be called upon in Britain to act as RECEIVER to handle the affairs of floundering companies or individuals.

Offshore banking. The part of a country's banking business that is denominated in foreign currencies and transacted between foreigners. (The expression can also embrace foreign currency transactions between foreigners and residents.) London is the world's biggest offshore banking centre. Although New York is also an important centre for international banking business, most of it cannot be described as offshore since it is denominated in dollars, New York's domestic currency.

Old Lady of Threadneedle Street. The affectionate nickname for the BANK OF ENGLAND. The name comes from a drawing by the famous eighteenth-century cartoonist James Gillray, which depicts the Prime Minister of the time, William Pitt the Younger, trying to pinch the Bank's GOLD from a chest which is being very firmly sat upon by an old lady. The Bank is the proud owner of the original signed cartoon.

Open account. Trade finance that is not backed by BILLS OF

EXCHANGE. Almost all trading within national boundaries is financed on open account.

Open account leaves the vendor at risk, since payment is by CHEQUE (which could bounce), by BANKER'S DRAFT, by MAIL TRANSFER or by TELEGRAPHIC TRANSFER. Suitable only when the seller trusts the buyer.

Open cheque. A CHEQUE that is not CROSSED. An open cheque can be exchanged in a bank for CASH. It is, therefore, more attractive to thieves than a crossed cheque, which can only be paid into a bank ACCOUNT. The bank handing over cash for an open cheque has no way of telling whether the recipient of the cash is the rightful owner of the cheque.

Open-end investment fund. An investment fund that is open in the sense that it issues new shares every time that it receives new money from investors – unlike a CLOSED-END INVESTMENT FUND, which issues a limited number of shares that are then traded only in a SECONDARY MARKET. In Britain open-end investment funds are called UNIT TRUSTS.

Open-market operations. Dealings by a CENTRAL BANK in the MONEY MARKET or SECURITIES market in order to adjust the amount of money and credit wandering around an economy. If the central bank buys securities, it pays for them with a CHEQUE. The receiver of the cheque puts it into his bank ACCOUNT, thereby increasing the total ASSETS of the bank (money). When the central bank sells securities it takes a cheque out of the banking system. The cheque disappears into a black hole at the central bank and, hey presto, the MONEY SUPPLY is reduced.

Opportunity cost. What an investor loses by not putting his money into an investment that would earn him a return. There is an opportunity cost every time you buy TRAVELLER'S CHEQUES or carry around CASH. The cost is the amount you could have earned if, instead of carrying the cash around, you had put it into, say, an INTEREST-earning DEPOSIT ACCOUNT.

Option. A contract which gives the holder the right to buy or sell an underlying SECURITY, commodity or currency before a certain date (see CALL OPTION and PUT OPTION). For example, an option to buy ICI shares at 100 pence before the end of April can be purchased for a small down–payment. If the share looks as if it will be below that price as the end of April approaches, then the option will not be exercised and the down–payment will be sacrificed. If the ICI share price is above 100 pence, then the option can be exercised and the shares delivered to the option holder. He can then sell them in the SPOT market at a profit.

Options are growing like mushrooms in the United States, with new contracts being devised almost daily. They enable investors to HEDGE their exposure to price movements and allow speculators to have a good old fling.

Organization for Economic Co-operation and Development (OECD). The Paris-based meeting place for twenty-four mostly rich, capitalist countries, viz. Australia, Austria, Belgium, Canada, Denmark, Finland, France, West Germany, Greece, Iceland, Ireland, Italy, Japan, LUXEMBOURG, the Netherlands, New Zealand, Norway, Portugal, Spain, Sweden, Switzerland, Turkey, the United Kingdom and the United States.

Apart from being a chat-house, the OECD is a great compiler of statistics on nearly every aspect of economic life in its member countries. It produces useful (if over-weighty) tomes on domestic and international CAPITAL MARKETS as well as its widely respected annual economic reports on each member country.

Overdraft. The peculiar European banking practice (rarely found in the United States or Japan) of giving borrowers a credit facility and then letting them draw on it as they will. Overdrafts are very popular with companies and individuals for their flexibility (once set up) and for allowing the borrower to pay for only as much as he wants to borrow. The alternative (common in the United States) is for a borrower to arrange a loan facility with his bank, for which he pays a COMMITMENT FEE whether he uses it or not.

Over-the-counter market. A market for SECURITIES that is outside any official STOCK EXCHANGE.

P

Paid-up capital. The amount paid by shareholders for a company's issued shares. Some of the shares may have been issued in partly paid form, in which case the paid-up CAPITAL will be less than the issued capital. Further calls may then be made on shareholders to fork out the rest at a later date.

The biggest public issue the London stockmarket has ever seen (for 51 per cent of the nationalized British Telecom) was sold in partly paid form, with two calls scheduled for one and two years respectively after the actual issue. Asking shareholders to come up all at once with the billions of pounds that the issue was designed to raise would not only have put many of them off buying but might also have done nasty things to the MONEY SUPPLY and to bank borrowing.

Par. Shares are said to be issued at par when they are sold at their FACE VALUE, as opposed to being sold at a discount to their face value.

Paribas. The French *banque d'affaires* (a sort of COMMERICAL-cum-MERCHANT BANK) nationalized in 1981. Its headquarters are in a splendid building in Paris where Napoleon married Josephine.

Paribas managed to sell off its big Swiss subsidiary to foreigners just before nationalization, much to the disgust of the socialist government. In 1984, however, the government bought back most of the Swiss subsidiary. In the same year Paribas set up the first VENTURE CAPITAL fund in France (a rather unsocialist thing to do).

Paris Club. An informal group of Western creditor governments who meet (usually in Paris), are chaired by the French Treasury and RESCHEDULE the loans they have made to developing countries that are no longer able to repay them on schedule. These loans include straight government-to-government credits and officially guaranteed EXPORT CREDITS.

Argentina was the first visitor to the club in 1956. Since then more than twenty countries have visited the club's favourite meeting place, the former Hotel Majestic on the Avenue Kléber. Many of them have come to Paris more than once. A few negotiations have been held outside Paris. The rescheduling talks with Peru in 1968, for example, were held in London.

Table 30 *Debt reschedulings at the Paris Club*

1956	Argentina
1959	Turkey
1961	Brazil
1962	Argentina
1963	—
1964	Brazil
1965	Argentina, Chile, Turkey
1966	Ghana, Indonesia
1967	Indonesia
1968	Ghana, India, Indonesia, Peru
1969	Peru
1970	Ghana, Indonesia
1971	India
1972	Chile, Khmer Republic, Pakistan
1973	India, Pakistan
1974	Chile, Ghana, India, Pakistan
1975	Chile, India
1976	India, Zaire
1977	India, Sierra Leone, Zaire
1978	Gabon, Peru, Turkey
1979	Sudan, Togo, Turkey, Zaire
1980	Liberia, Sierra Leone, Turkey
1981	Central African Republic, Liberia, Madagascar, Pakistan, Senegal, Togo, Uganda, Zaire
1982	Madagascar, Malawi, Senegal, Sudan, Uganda
1983	Brazil, Costa Rica, Cuba, Ecuador, Liberia, Malawi, Mexico, Morocco, Niger, Peru, Senegal, Sudan, Togo, Zaire, Zambia

Source: OECD.

Park Avenue. The posh street that runs north to south on New York's Manhattan island and whose midriff is home to a host of COMMERCIAL BANKS, both American and foreign. Park Avenue gives New York two FINANCIAL CENTRES, the other being WALL STREET at the tip of the island.

Participation. Joining in new ISSUES of SECURITIES or new loans by banks at the lower levels – i.e. after all the big fee-earning jobs in UNDERWRITING or SYNDICATING have been parcelled out.

Passbook. An old-fashioned way of keeping account of a bank ACCOUNT. It is still the method used by most of Britain's BUILDING SOCIETIES and by SAVINGS BANKS around the world. A passbook is a book retained by a depositor or borrower in which entries are made to record his or her deposits, repayments and withdrawals. Automation now tolls the death knell of the passbook system.

Pawnbroker. Recognized for centuries in Britain by the fast-disappearing sign of the three golden balls hanging outside their premises, pawnbrokers are bankers to the poor and the about-to-be poor. They lend money on the SECURITY of property (e.g. jewellery, hi-fi) deposited with them. The loan is inevitably much lower than the value of the property.

If borrowers repay the money (and the INTEREST due) within six months, they can get their property back. If they don't, the pawnbroker has the right to sell the goods.

Penn Square Bank. The small bank in Oklahoma that, when it collapsed in 1982 from a surfeit of loans to over-wild wildcatters, broke a bank in old Chicago (CONTINENTAL ILLINOIS).

Performance bond. A GUARANTEE from a bank to an importer (often provided by the exporter's bank) that the exporter will fulfil his contract according to its terms and conditions; often used in the construction industry (particularly in the Middle East) when the buyer wants some hold over the construction company to ensure that it completes a project on time and as promised.

A failure to perform according to the terms of the BOND will then give the buyer some degree of financial compensation for the delay or failure to meet the specifications.

Personal Identification Number (PIN). The number needed by every plastic card holder to enable him to get at his bank ACCOUNT through an AUTOMATED TELLER MACHINE or some similar such manifestation of electronic banking. Usually sent secretly in a brown envelope separately from the plastic card itself, PIN numbers in Britain have four digits and are a great nuisance. Remembering them is not easy. The alternative – carrying them around but keeping them apart from the plastic card – is almost as difficult. Should a thief get hold of your plastic card and its accompanying PIN number, he could, of course, make hay with your account. Maybe CHEQUES are better.

Personal loan. A bank loan to an individual in which the INTEREST and PRINCIPAL are bundled together and repaid in equal monthly instalments over a period that may reach five years. RATES of interest on personal loans are often painfully high.

Pink sheet. Sheets that are printed daily in the United States on pink paper. On them are listed all the BROKERS who make markets in OVER-THE-COUNTER stocks and AMERICAN DEPOSITARY RECEIPTS.

Pit. The part of a trading floor where FUTURES contracts are bought and sold amid much hand waving and screaming. Perversely, pits are raised, not sunken.

Portfolio. A collection of financial ASSETS belonging to a single owner. A diversified portfolio will contain things like SECURITIES, bank deposits, GOLD and BILLS, on the principle that the more diverse the assets, the lower the RISK.

Post-dated cheque. A CHEQUE with a future date written on it. The payee of a post-dated cheque cannot get the cheque paid to him or her until that future date. Before then the payer can always cancel the cheque.

Post Office. In many countries governments use branches of the Post Office system to collect state savings deposits (NATIONAL SAVINGS in Britain) and to provide a counter service for postal GIRO. In Japan almost one-third of all personal savings are collected through the Post Office.

Pre-emptive bid. A bid for a company that is set at a high price with the aim of discouraging any subsequent counter-bidders.

Preference shares. Shares which give their owner a fixed DIVIDEND, as opposed to ordinary shares whose dividend depends on the profits of the company. Preference shareholders have a right to their dividend before any payment is made to the ordinary shareholders. If a company goes bust, preference shareholders are entitled to a maximum of the nominal value of their shares. Ordinary shareholders get whatever is left over after that.

Preferential creditor. A creditor of a company who, if the company goes bust, has a preferential claim on whatever ASSETS are left, over and above the claims of ordinary creditors.

Premium. The regular payment to an insurer for providing insurance cover, be it for a life, a ship or a wedding ring.

A premium is also the amount paid over and above some mathematical calculation of a value (e.g. for a company over and above its MARKET VALUE, or for a FUTURES contract over and above the SPOT PRICE).

Price/earnings (P/E) ratio. The famous ratio that is supposed to be the acid test of whether a company's shares are undervalued. It is the ratio of a company's stockmarket value (i.e. its number of shares multiplied by its share price) to its latest annual earnings (i.e. its after-tax profit). To say the same thing in another way: it is the number of years it would take an investor to get his money back if the company kept its profits constant and distributed all of them every year. Of course, companies do neither. So P/E ratios vary wildly and depend on all sorts of factors (e.g. the omnipresent 'expectations').

Primary dealers. The thirty-seven American financial institutions (including some big banks) authorized to buy new government SECURITIES direct from the US Treasury. Primary dealers are also secondary dealers making markets in outstanding US government securities (see SECONDARY MARKET). They are, however, but a small percentage of all secondary dealers.

Primary market. The market in which fresh new SECURITIES (or, indeed, any other financial ASSET that can subsequently be resold) are first sold. It contrasts with the SECONDARY MARKET, the market for second-hand assets that have already been owned by someone else.

Prime rate. The key borrowing RATE in the United States. The rate that top-class corporate borrowers (like, say, IBM) pay their banks for SHORT-TERM loans. When banks have more money to lend than they know what to do with, they will sometimes lend to the very best borrowers at rates below prime.

Principal. The FACE VALUE of a loan. To be distinguished from INTEREST, which is what you pay every year for the principal. On LONG-TERM loans interest soon outstrips principal repayments. Look at any MORTGAGE loan and see how much is being paid in interest and how much in principal.

Private bank. A bank that is owned by a limited number of partners (fewer than twenty in Britain), each of whom bears UNLIMITED LIABILITY for the debts of the bank. There are more surviving private banks in continental Europe than in Anglo-Saxon countries. Since they do not have to report publicly too many details of their business, private banks are very popular in secretive Switzerland.

Private Export Funding Corporation (PEFCO). An American company that specializes in providing LONG-TERM export finance when backed by a GUARANTEE from EXIMBANK. PEFCO is owned by a lot of banks (over fifty) plus a smaller number of companies that are not banks.

Private placing. The sale of a large part of a new ISSUE (or of existing shares) to a small group of investors – usually big institutions like insurance companies and pension funds. The sale is private in the sense that it is not offered to the general public and does not pass across the floor of a STOCK EXCHANGE.

Privatization. The sale to the private sector, by a government, of businesses that have sometimes been taken from the private sector by another government. All the rage in Mrs Thatcher's Britain.

Britain's biggest privatization took place in 1984: the sale of 51 per cent of British Telecom, originally expected to raise around £4 billion, the biggest single transaction the London CAPITAL MARKETS have ever seen. Banks get involved in advising governments on the best way to sell these bits and pieces. KLEINWORT BENSON and S. G. WARBURG had the task of making British Telecom as digestible as possible.

Table 31 *British privatization*[1]

1979–80	£m	%	1982–83	£m	%
British Petroleum	276	5.18	Britoil shares	627	51
National Enterprise	37	—	Associated British Ports	46	49
Drake & Scull Holdings	1	—	British Rail Hotels	34	100
Suez Finance Company	22	—	International Aeradio	60	100
1980–81			1983–84		
British Aerospace	43	50	Scott Lithgow Shipyard	—	100
National Enterprise	83	—	Cable & Wireless	263	22
1981–82			British Petroleum	543	7.1
British Sugar Corporation	44	16	1984–85		
Cable & Wireless	182	49	Associated British Ports	51	48.5
Amersham International	64	100	Enterprise Oil	392	100
National Freight Company	5	100	Inmos	95	76
National Enterprise	2	—	Sealink	66	100
British Petroleum	8	—	Jaguar	293	100

Note:
[1] by financial year.

Pro forma invoice. A sort of first stab at getting an export order. The first draft of an exporter's bill to an importer, the pro forma invoice contains estimated prices on the basis of which the importer decides whether he wants to confirm an order or not.

Project finance. A way of financing big capital projects (like dams, generators or mines), which depends for its security on the expected CASH FLOW of the project itself rather than on GUARANTEES from third parties (like governments) or the borrower.

Promissory note. A legally binding promise between two parties that one will pay the other a stated amount at a future date.

Prospectus. A document which outlines a company's plans, in particular when it is offering shares for sale to the public. In Britain the contents of a prospectus offering shares for sale are laid down in the Companies Act of 1948. STOCK EXCHANGES have their own additional requirements.

Protectionism. An emotive word used to refer to any barriers to trade that the user disapproves of. Protectionism had a big hand in the 60 per cent decline in the volume of world trade between 1929 and 1932. That almost led to the total collapse of the world's FINANCIAL SYSTEM. Protectionism is rearing its ugly head again today.

Developing countries, under pressure to boost their exports to help service their debts, are finding more and more barriers to their goods in rich Western countries. The rich complain that the poor are unfairly dumping subsidized goods and threatening to destroy their own domestic industries. But if developing countries do not export enough, they will not repay their debts. And that threatens to destroy rich countries' banks. A stark choice for the rich: your money or your shirts (your banks or your textile factories).

Provisions. Money that banks set aside, out of their earnings, against a rainy day. Most provisions are calculated as a percentage of a bank's loans to doubtful debtors (borrowers who look as if they might not in future be able to repay their loans in full). Banks have not yet set aside much against the biggest doubtful debtors of them all – Latin American countries. However, practices in different countries vary. West German and Swiss banks are believed to have made the most generous provisions against developing-country loans, American banks the least generous.

British banks make two sorts of provisions: specific and general. Specific provisions are set aside against specific identifiable borrowers who look dicey. General provisions are not linked to individual borrowers; they are based on a hunch about what expected market conditions might mean for borrowers who cannot yet be identified as dicey. The BANK OF ENGLAND includes general (but not specific) provisions as part of a bank's CAPITAL in its calculations of banks' PRUDENTIAL RATIOS.

American banks, which disclose most information about their provisions, have been increasing them dramatically in recent years. In 1982 their provisions were over 60 per cent higher than the year before. Most of the increase was to cover domestic problems in the oil and property markets. The first American banks to make provisions of more than $100 million in a quarter (the second three months of 1982) were BANK OF AMERICA, SEAFIRST and CONTINENTAL ILLINOIS. Since then three other American banks have made quarterly provisions of over $100 million. The record so far is held by the Texas bank InterFirst, which set aside a staggering $430.3 million in the third quarter of 1983.

Proxy fight. An American technique for gaining control of a company (or inducing it to make some major change) without actually paying for it. A small group of shareholders lobbies the rest to hand it their PROXY VOTES to enable the group either to make the change or to vote some of its own representatives on to the board of the company.

Proxy vote. How to wield influence at company meetings without actually being there. A proxy vote is a vote delegated to somebody else by the person authorized to cast it. Often used by company shareholders who cannot attend an annual or EXTRAORDINARY GENERAL MEETING.

Prudential ratios. The ratios that regulators consider it is prudent for banks to maintain between different items on their balance sheet (see CAPITAL RATIO and LIQUIDITY RATIO). In some countries prudential ratios are rigidly laid down in statute; in others they are left flexible, to be interpreted and enforced by CENTRAL BANKS or other supervisors.

In Britain and Japan a third ratio is watched closely: the free capital ratio, the amount of a bank's CAPITAL that is not tied up in fixed ASSETS (e.g. land and buildings).

Public company. A company that offers its shares for sale to the general public – as opposed to a private company that is owned by a small group, often members of one family. A private company may 'go public' by a new ISSUE of its shares. If its shares then get a LISTING on a recognized STOCK EXCHANGE, it becomes a QUOTED COMPANY.

Put option. The right to sell a currency or SECURITY at a stated price (the STRIKE PRICE) within a fixed period of time. If the strike price is higher than the price in the SPOT market, the holder of the option will buy the currency (or security) and exercise his option at a profit (the difference between the strike price and the spot market price).

Q

Quoted company. A company whose share price is quoted on a recognized STOCK EXCHANGE. To obtain a quotation (i.e. to be quoted on an exchange) a company will have to meet certain standards laid down by the exchange. Thereafter it will have to maintain prescribed levels of disclosure. In return, the exchange makes the company's shares marketable by providing a price and a place where buyers and sellers can meet.

R

Rabobank Nederland. The CENTRAL BANK for a large number of small regional CO-OPERATIVE BANKS in the Netherlands. The co-operative banks are known as Raiffeisen banks after the Prussian Friedrich Raiffeisen, who first set up a rural co-operative bank in the nineteenth century.

More than 40 per cent of the Netherlands' savings deposits are channelled thrugh the Raiffeisen banks, of which there are almost 1,000 with over 3,000 offices. They behave as fairly normal COMMERCIAL BANKS but with a strong slant towards agricultural business. Because they are small, Rabobank has been set up to pool their surplus resources and to do large-scale lending and international business for the whole group. Rabobank can also use its funds to help any one of the individual Raiffeisen banks that gets into trouble.

Radcliffe Report. The report of a committee chaired by a judge (Lord Radcliffe) and set up in 1957 to investigate the workings of the British monetary system. It recommended greater use of credit controls and less use of monetary ones. Until the WILSON REPORT appeared in 1980, it was the best description of the workings of the British FINANCIAL SYSTEM.

Rate. The price of money: either to borrow it (the INTEREST rate) or to exchange it for someone else's money (the exchange rate).

Rating. A simple way of indicating the chances that the repayment of INTEREST and PRINCIPAL by a borrower will be made on time. In the United States rating is big business, dominated by two companies – Moodys and Standard & Poor's. They give ratings to the specific debt of individual companies and grade it along the lines of a university essay, AAA (triple A) being the closest thing to perfection, C being just about the worst short of BANKRUPTCY. D is for debt that is actually in DEFAULT.

Ratings matter to companies because the higher their rating, the lower their cost of borrowing. In early 1984 AAA corporate bonds in America were YIELDING just over 12 per cent, while BBB corporate BONDS were yielding more than 13.25 per cent.

Real estate investment trust (REIT). An American INVESTMENT TRUST that invests in property development. REITs got themselves a bad name in the second half of the 1970s. When property prices dropped, several of them went bust, almost bringing down some banks with them.

Real rate of return. The difference between the actual rate of return from an investment and some specified measure of the rate of inflation. The real rate of return can be positive or negative.

Real time. When used in the context of electronic banking the expression refers to the ability of the system to update an ACCOUNT instantly as instructions are fed into a terminal (i.e. an AUTOMATED TELLER MACHINE, an EFTPOS terminal, etc.). It differs from the first generation of electronic banking systems in which instructions given to the terminal were stored for retrieval by the bank at its leisure. Such non-real-time systems were more susceptible to fraud. Money could be withdrawn from an account before the bank could discover that there was none left to be withdrawn.

Receivables. Money owing to a company and yet to be received. A figure closely watched by a company's bankers. If it increases too fast, the company can be in trouble, even though it is trading as well as ever.

Receiver. Someone (usually an accountant or a solicitor) called in by a troubled company's creditors to try to sort out the company's financial problems. The receiver's aim is to get the company back on the straight and narrow without its going into liquidation.

In Britain those authorized to call in a receiver are DEBENTURE holders with a FLOATING CHARGE over a company's ASSETS – almost invariably banks. To rectify this imbalance, and to give a company's other creditors a chance to get the same treatment, the British government proposes to introduce a new type of receiver called an ADMINISTRATOR. When close to INSOLVENCY, the company itself or any of its creditors will be able to apply to a court to appoint an administrator.

Reciprocity. The theory, much favoured in the United States, that FOREIGN BANKS from country B should be allowed to do only as much inside country A as country A's banks are allowed to do inside country B. Reciprocity would be ideal if all countries were equal. Since they are not, small countries balk at the idea of allowing themselves to be overrun by big American banks for the dubious privilege of being able to set up a branch in New York.

Recognized bank. The BANK OF ENGLAND allows two types of bank to operate in Britain: recognized banks and LICENSED DEPOSIT-TAKING INSTITUTIONS. Recognized banks are allowed to carry out a wider range of banking business. In return they have to provide the Bank of England with greater assurances of their expertise and standing in the market. The Bank has been at great pains to point out that although there are two tiers of banking approval, there are not two classes of bank, upper and lower. There are now about 290 recognized banks in Britain – few of them British.

Reconciliation. The process of checking a company's own record of its financial transactions with that of its bankers, allowing for uncleared CHEQUES that are yet to be paid in or out.

Recycling. What banks do all the time, although the term refers specifically to what they did in the oil crisis of 1973/74: the taking of money from those with too much of it in order to lend it to those with too little. When the Organization of Petroleum Exporting Countries (OPEC) pushed up its prices in 1973, it increased its foreign exchange revenues way beyond the OPEC member countries' ability to spend it. On the other hand, non-oil-producing countries had to find extra foreign exchange to continue to buy the oil they needed. This they got from banks, the biggest recipients of the early OPEC surpluses. The loans that banks exuberantly made to these non-oil-producers came home to roost nine years later in the shape of the developing-country debt crisis.

Red clause. A clause typed in red in a LETTER OF CREDIT allowing the exporter to receive all the amount due on credit and in advance (sometimes) of the goods even being shipped. Red clauses originated with the Australian wool trade to enable well-known wool shippers to pay inland farmers before their wool was exported.

Red herring. A preliminary PROSPECTUS filed with the USA's SECURITIES AND EXCHANGE COMMISSION to test the market's reaction to a proposed new ISSUE of SECURITIES. The red herring contains a limited amount of information. It includes the number of shares to be issued but excludes any indication of the price.

Redemption. The exchange of SECURITIES for CASH or, maybe, for other securities at the time they MATURE – i.e. on redemption. The redemption dates on government securities are the dates between which the securities are redeemable at PAR.

Reference. What every new customer of a bank requires – the written opinion of someone who is already a good bank customer that the aspiring customer too will help the bank to make profits, not losses. A banker's reference is different. It is a brief letter written in veiled bankerspeak and giving an assessment of the creditworthiness of someone with whom the customer of another bank is about to do business.

Reference bank. A bank whose INTEREST RATES are used as a base for determining the rates on a loan or other form of credit.

Refinancing. Paying off existing debt with new (and cheaper) loans. As INTEREST RATES fall, all borrowers want to REFINANCE their FIXED-RATE debt if possible. Only some succeed. In many cases banks impose penalty clauses for the early repayment of debt. Even with these penalty clauses, refinancing may still make good financial sense.

Borrowers sometimes get into a semantic discussion as to whether they are refinancing their debt (clever) or RESCHEDULING their debt (not very clever).

Refunding. Replacing one ISSUE of government debt with another as the first one comes to MATURITY. Holders of the old SECURITIES are sometimes offered new ones in a straight exchange.

Regional Cheque Processing Centre (RCPC). In the United

States, where there are more than 14,000 banks, the clearing of CHEQUES drawn on one bank and presented at another is a complex problem. The country is organized into forty-six different RCPCs to facilitate cheque-clearing; thirty-four of the RCPCs are at the branches of the various federal reserve banks. (See FEDERAL RESERVE BOARD.)

Registered security. A debt issued by a company to a buyer whose name is registered with the company. When the SECURITY changes hands the name of its new owner has to be recorded on the company's register. In the United States most securities have to be issued in registered form – which is why many investors prefer EUROBONDS to American domestic BONDS. Eurobonds are BEARER BONDS and belong to whoever carries them. That way their owners can remain anonymous.

Regulation. Not only what bank supervisors do to banks, but also the binding laws of the EUROPEAN ECONOMIC COMMUNITY. They prescribe the time limits within which member states must introduce Community rules into their own domestic legislation.

Regulation Q. The infamous American rule which allowed the FEDERAL RESERVE BOARD to set limits on the RATES which banks could pay to most types of depositor. As Regulation Q rates became more and more out of line with market rates in the 1970s, banks found they were losing out to financial institutions that were not constrained by the Fed's rules. So Regulation Q finally got thrown out of the window in 1983.

Remittance. Money sent from one country to another; often the earnings of migrant workers sent from their place of work to their families in their country of origin. For some countries, like Turkey, India and the Philippines, remittances are a major source of foreign currency earnings – and good business for their banks.

Repos. Shorthand for sale and repurchase agreements, an American device for smoothing the passage of government SECURITIES into the hands of investors. Repos are contracts between (usually) a BROKER and a bank or company with some surplus cash. The bank (it can be a federal reserve bank – see

FEDERAL RESERVE BOARD) buys the securities and agrees to sell them back at a future date (a few days hence) at an agreed price. By the time the securities are returned to the broker he has (with luck) found a LONG-TERM investor to buy them. Around 70 per cent of at least one big US government securities sale in 1984 was sold initially in the form of repos.

Representative office. The smallest formal presence that a bank can have in a foreign country. A representative office does no lending or deposit-taking. It merely looks after the interests in the foreign country of the bank's customers back home. Sometimes the 'office' is no more than a part-time employee and a telephone.

Rescheduling. Putting off until tomorrow what you cannot pay today. Done most publicly by developing countries and their bankers, but often less publicly by other willing creditors and debtors – e.g. governments (see PARIS CLUB), banks and companies, or even the Electricity Board and impoverished consumers.

Table 32 *Debt rescheduling 1975–83*

Country	Number of reschedulings	Total value ($ bn)	By government	By bank
Mexico	2	24.55	2.00	22.55
Brazil	2	13.60	3.80	9.80
Turkey	5	10.44	4.70	5.74
Poland	n.a.	8.10	2.20	5.90
Argentina	2	6.97	—	6.97
Chile	2	4.32	0.22	4.10
Zaire	6	4.17	3.77	0.40
Peru	4	4.07	0.93	3.14
Yugoslavia	1	3.80	—	3.80
Romania	4	2.55	0.43	2.12
Total (including others)	84	98.60	23.46	75.14

Source: OECD.

Reserve(s). What a company keeps 'in reserve'. Reserves are built up mostly from retained profits, i.e. profits that are not distributed to shareholders as DIVIDENDS. Technically, reserves belong to the shareholders and are kept by the company as a buffer to meet any unexpectedly heavy expenditure (like buying another company or hard times). Banks have to maintain reserves at levels ordained by their supervisors.

Reserve asset ratio. The ratio that a bank in Britain formerly had to maintain between its ELIGIBLE LIABILITIES and its RESERVE ASSETS. Between 1971 and January 1981 the ratio was 12.5 per cent; it went down to 10 per cent, then to 8 per cent, before being abolished altogether in August 1981. Since then the BANK OF ENGLAND has used other ratios to reassure itself that its charges are sufficiently LIQUID to meet any unsuspected demand from customers for their deposits.

Reserve assets. Those ASSETS of banks in Britain which the BANK OF ENGLAND once considered to be sufficiently LIQUID to be convertible quickly into CASH and to count towards their RESERVE ASSET RATIO. Reserve assets included cash itself, most deposits held with the Bank of England, Treasury BILLS and some other SECURITIES which the Bank of England was prepared to DISCOUNT as and when necessary.

Reserve bank. See CENTRAL BANK.

Reserve currency. Currencies in which CENTRAL BANKS are happy to denominate their RESERVES – i.e. the dollar, the Deutschmark, the yen (if they could get their hands on it) and, occasionally, the Swiss franc, the pound and the French franc. Some countries (like Japan) do not like their currencies to be used as reserve currencies on the grounds that it makes their exchange RATES more volatile and reduces domestic control over those rates. To get over some of these objections, artificial reserve currencies like SPECIAL DRAWING RIGHTS and the EUROPEAN CURRENCY UNIT have been created. They are little more than a basket of the sorts of currencies that countries would want to hold in their reserves.

Residual maturity. See MATURITY.

Retail banking. That part of banking most visible to the man in the street; the business of providing services to individuals and small companies. Retail banking has three special features:
- It deals with large volumes of low-value transactions.
- It has traditionally been provided through large networks of branches that are becoming less and less economically justifiable.
- New technology (such as AUTOMATED TELLER MACHINES and HOME BANKING) is transforming the ways in which it can be marketed.

Returns. CHEQUES which for one reason or another are sent back to the bank branch at which they were originally presented. The reason may simply be that they were incorrectly filled in.

Revolving credit. A loan in which, as soon as any bit is repaid, that bit can immediately be borrowed again. A revolving credit has an upper limit to the amount that can be borrowed but no limit to the number of times that amount can be reached (assuming that some of it has been repaid in the meantime).

Rights issue. A new ISSUE of company SECURITIES offered first to existing holders of the company's securities at a DISCOUNT to their market price. Sometimes those who do not take up their rights make their shares available to the general public; sometimes the shares are just not issued. In Britain the majority of new share issues by QUOTED companies are in the form of rights issues.

Riksbank. Sweden's CENTRAL BANK with a good claim to being the oldest central bank in the world. It was founded in 1668 as the Rikets Standers Bank, 'the bank of the estates of the realm'.

Ring. That part of the LONDON METAL EXCHANGE where trading takes place.

Risk. What bankers get paid for taking; the danger inherent in taking money in one form from person A and lending it in another form to person B. The different ways in which deposits get mutated into loans give rise to different risks, so there are:

- Exchange risks, from, say, taking dollar deposits and making sterling loans.
- INTEREST-RATE risks from, say, taking deposits linked to LIBOR and making FIXED-RATE loans.
- MATURITY risks, from, say, taking deposits with seven days' notice of withdrawal and making loans not repayable for one year.
- Political risks, from, say, collecting dollars in the USA to lend to Argentina.
- Credit risks, from, say, taking dollars from the IBM Corporation to lend to the IB Doubtful Corporation.

Risk-averse. The extent to which an investor is reluctant to take a RISK. Banks are traditionally risk-averse because they are handling the money of people (depositors) who expect to get their original deposit back in full – plus some. VENTURE CAPITAL funds and investments that make no prior commitment to a particular RATE of return can affort to be less risk-averse.

Roll-over. The practice of extending a loan beyond its original final payment date. Many developing countries got into bad habits in the 1970s because they assumed that their SHORT-TERM bank loans would be rolled over indefinitely and would become LONG-TERM loans. When banks decided to stop this process

(because they lost confidence in the developing countries' ability to repay them) they precipitated the international debt dramas of the 1980s. Rolling over was big enough for Jane Fonda to make a movie about it.

Rothschild, N. M. The London MERCHANT BANK that carries one of the most famous names in banking. It no longer has any links with the French bank of the same name, started by the brothers of Nathan Mayer Rothschild, the nineteenth-century founder of the London bank. The French bank is now nationalized, and N. M. Rothschild changed from a partnership to a company in 1970.

N. M. Rothschild is strong in corporate finance and is one of the five GOLD dealers who FIX the London gold bullion price.

Roundtripping. A neat way for companies in Britain to make money when INTEREST RATE differentials work in a particular way. On occasion, British OVERDRAFT rates for top companies are lower than rates in the MONEY MARKETS. At such times a company can use all the overdraft facilities it was agreed on with its bankers, and place the money back into the money markets. It then makes a TURN on the difference in the interest rates merely by sending the money on a roundtrip out of the bank, into the company, into the money market and back into the bank again.

Royal Bank of Scotland. Scotland's biggest bank and the only one of the big three that is proudly independent of the dreaded Sassenach (the BANK OF SCOTLAND is 35 per cent owned by BARCLAYS, and CLYDESDALE is wholly owned by MIDLAND). In fact, the Royal Bank owns an English CLEARING BANK, Williams & Glyn's, which has about 320 branches in England and Wales and 3 per cent of the London clearing banks' total deposits. The Royal Bank claims about 45 per cent of the saturated Scottish banking market.

In 1981 the Royal Bank nearly fell into foreign hands. After a fierce takeover battle between Standard Chartered and the HONGKONG AND SHANGHAI BANKING CORPORATION, it was saved from their clutches by the MONOPOLIES AND MERGERS COMMISSION, which ruled that neither bank was a suitable suitor. That left the Royal Bank wondering what to do and where to go next.

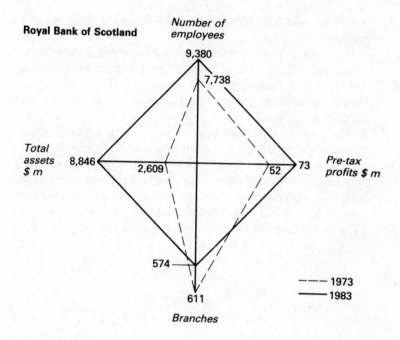

Royal Bank of Scotland

Number of employees

9,380

7,738

Total assets $ m — 8,846 — 2,609 — 52 — 73 — *Pre-tax profits $ m*

574

611

Branches

--- 1973
— 1983

Rumasa. The Spanish conglomerate taken over by the Spanish government in February 1983. Rumasa was a jumble of hotels, wine and sherry makers, and banks – lots of them. The biggest and most profitable bank was Banco Atlantico, eventually sold off by the government to a Spanish/Arab consortium.

Rumasa brought universal fame to its chairman, Mr José Maria Ruiz-Mateus, whose family owned most of the company. He fled to London and pleaded his cause of unjust expropriation, ultimately unsuccessfully. In April 1984 he was detained in Frankfurt pending extradition back to Spain on several criminal charges, including the violation of foreign exchange controls.

Run. Two meanings:
• As in a 'run on the bank', the stuff of which bankers' nightmares are made: depositors stampeding to their nearest branch to get their money out as fast as possible because they do not think it will be available much longer – a self-fulfilling fear. The more depositors withdraw their money, the less money there is to

withdraw and the more depositors there are who want to withdraw it.

Runs were more common in the nineteenth than in the twentieth century – the spice of many a Victorian melodrama. Nowadays in most developed countries DEPOSIT PROTECTION FUNDS and sophisticated CENTRAL BANKS can stop runs before they become dangerous.

● The small group of nine of America's ten biggest banks whose CERTIFICATES OF DEPOSIT are interchangeable among dealers – i.e. the dealer does not even look at the name on the certificate if it is issued by one of them. CONTINENTAL ILLINOIS suffered the ignominy of being dropped from this run after it got landed with a whole load of bad loans from the BANKRUPT PENN SQUARE BANK. Later it also had to endure the other sort of run.

S

Salomon Brothers. The investment bank that is currently the USA's top UNDERWRITER by far, having raised more capital for American companies in 1983 and the first quarter of 1984 than its two nearest rivals put together.

Salomon Brothers was bought by the commodity dealer Phibro in 1981. The merger has been an uneasy one, as Salomon Brothers' performance has outstripped that of its new parent. When absorbed by Phibro, Salomon Brothers was a 71-year-old partnership that specialized in BLOCK TRADING and institutional BROKERage business. It is now the second biggest WALL STREET INVESTMENT BANK (in terms of its CAPITALIZATION) – second only to the mighty MERRILL LYNCH.

Samurai bond. The Japanese version of YANKEE BONDS and BULLDOG BONDS. A yen-denominated bond issued in Japan by a non-Japanese borrower.

Sarakin. Unregulated Japanese HIRE-PURCHASE outfits unashamedly referred to in Japan as loan sharks. Because Japan's domestic INTEREST RATES are tightly controlled, credit is allocated not by price (i.e. interest rate) but by government edict. Banks give industry first priority, and consumers have a hard time finding bank loans to buy washing machines, televisions, etc. Enter the *sarakin* to meet their needs, but at outrageously inflated rates of interest – up to 100 per cent per annum in 1983, when Japan's inflation rate was a mere 1.8 per cent. The government is trying to crack down on the *sarakin*. Their rough tactics were deemed to be the cause of 813 suicides in 1983.

Satellite banking. A way of organizing bank branches that is not as much in vogue as it once was. Satellite branches are clustered in groups around a main branch. The satellites provide a limited range of services, while big and complicated business is referred to the big branch. Trouble is, if a customer calls on his local branch, only to be told to go to see a bigger branch in a distant town, he may go to a nearby competitor bank that has not organized itself into a satellite system and can give him what he wants on the spot.

Saudi Arabian Monetary Agency (SAMA). The nearest thing

Saudi Arabia has to a CENTRAL BANK. Extremely secretive and powerful, it has had much of the country's huge oil revenues to invest. Its investments have been mostly SHORT-TERM – the likes of American TREASURY BILLS and deposits with a select list of Western banks. This list was once a closely guarded secret, believed to contain about twenty names. However, as banks grow more disenchanted with international lending, they grow less keen on taking SAMA's huge deposits. So the list has become longer and less exclusive. SAMA's main concern now is with the internationalization of the Saudi currency (the *riyal*) via OFFSHORE BANKS in BAHRAIN. In 1984 Saudi Arabia introduced (for the first time) its own version of a Treasury bill to mop up some of the surplus LIQUIDITY of the domestic Saudi banks. (A standard type of Treasury bill would have offended Islamic laws on usury.)

Savings and loan association (S. & L.). Close American cousins of Britain's BUILDING SOCIETIES. The S. & L.s are America's main (but not only) MORTGAGE lenders. They got in a terrible mess in 1981/82 (in the two years their aggregate losses were $8.6 billion) because they differed in one important respect from Britain's building societies: they offered LONG-TERM mortgages at FIXED

Table 33 *Largest American savings and loan associations*

	Home town	Deposits $ b, Dec 31st	
		1983	1982
American Savings	Beverly Hills	18.26	6.24
Home Savings of America	Los Angeles	15.51	11.83
Great Western Savings	Beverly Hills	18.26	8.75
California	Los Angeles	11.06	7.57
Glendale	Glendale	7.51	6.78
Empire of America	Buffalo	5.87	3.21
First Nationwide Savings	San Francisco	5.85	4.48
World Savings	Oakland	5.77	4.84
Home	San Diego	5.09	4.53
Talman Home	Chicago	5.07	5.07

Source: Federal Home Loan Bank Board, American Banker.

RATES of INTEREST. (Building societies' rates are FLOATING RATES.) When America's deposit rates were DEREGULATED (and rose astronomically), the S. & L.s were stuck with low-rate loans while paying high rates for their deposits.

Amazingly, they survived that problem, even though many of them became technically INSOLVENT in the meanwhile, and some of them folded (264 in 1982, 175 in 1983, including the Empire S. & L. of Mesquite, Texas, which had grown by 1,685 per cent in two years – something of a record). The S. & L.s have gradually shifted their ASSETS into floating-rate mortgages and begun to do new types of business as new legislation, concerned about their fate, has given them wider powers.

Though many have merged and some have been taken over by banks, the S. & L.s are now in better health. In 1983 the 4,000-odd survivors lent $138 billion in home loans (an all-time record). Some expected 1984's figure to be 40 per cent higher.

The S. & L.s are regulated by the FEDERAL HOME LOAN BANK BOARD or by their local state banking department. (See also THRIFTS.)

Savings bank. In olden times a bank which accepted only the deposits of small savers, did no business with industry and provided no money-transmission service. These distinctions between savings banks and other banks are now being eroded.

Table 34 *The savings of America*
(savings deposits in federally insured institutions: $b)

	Commercial Banks	Savings Banks	Savings & Loan Associations
1975	161	70	286
1976	204	67	336
1977	220	70	387
1978	221	64	431
1979	207	54	470
1980	201	47	512
1981	224	44	525
1982	305	49	566
1983	438	67	632

Source: FDIC, Federal Home Loan Bank Board.

Savings banks, like others, are becoming all-in-one banks. Britain's TRUSTEE SAVINGS BANKS, for example, now lend to industry, give personal loans, provide CHEQUE books and CREDIT CARDS and offer all the paraphernalia of full COMMERICAL BANKS.

Scrip issue. A gift of free shares to a company's existing shareholders in proportion to their stake in the company. A scrip issue merely converts a company's RESERVES (which belonged to the shareholders anyway) into share CAPITAL – confirming once again the old adage that there is no such thing as a free share. A scrip issue is little more than an accounting device. Although shareholders end up with more shares, their MARKET VALUE adjusts to reflect the fact. Shareholders end up with more shares, worth *in toto* more or less the same.

Seafirst. A large bank in Washington state that did very well until it decided in the late 1970s to splurge into energy lending in Oklahoma. It splurged so far that when the loans were unpaid it had to be bailed out (in 1983) by California's BANK OF AMERICA. Bank of America was given special dispensation to cross the state boundary.

Sears Roebuck. The world's largest retailer, which could soon be the world's largest FINANCIAL SUPERMARKET. Based in Chicago, with its headquarters in the tallest building on earth, the 110-storey Sears Tower, the company has recently begun to sell financial services as if they were groceries. It bought a MORTGAGE bank, Coldwell Banker, and a BROKERage firm, Dean Witter Reynolds, at a time when such combinations were illegal for pure banking companies. With its phenomenal marketing power, Sears Roebuck has made America's biggest banks quake.

Seasonal borrowing. A privilege granted to smaller American banks that are members of the FEDERAL RESERVE BOARD. It allows them to borrow from the system to smooth out seasonal fluctuations in their balance sheets. Big banks are not granted the privilege because they can do their smoothing in the MONEY MARKET, to which smaller banks do not have access.

Secondary banking crisis. A dangerous time in British banking

Sears Roebuck (see p. 164)

history. In 1974 a number of small, inadequately regulated banks got burned by the collapse of property prices. For a moment (it seemed longer), they threatened to bring down a bevy of perfectly sound banks with them. The BANK OF ENGLAND stepped in and organized the LIFEBOAT to bail out the good and the just – and some others not so good or so just. The crisis scarred the memory of many a banker still working in the CITY.

Secondary market. The market in second-hand financial instruments like shares, BONDS, or CERTIFICATES OF DEPOSIT. When first issued, these instruments are sold in the PRIMARY MARKET. Much of their initial attraction for buyers lies in the knowledge that there is a secondary market in which their investment can be resold (albeit sometimes at a loss).

Secrecy. A commodity much prized by Third World politicians, Swiss drug companies and American drug runners. The darkest secrecy is reputed to be obtained from Swiss banks, but countries like Austria, Lichtenstein and the CAYMAN ISLANDS sometimes boast that they have more to offer to the nervous rich.

The Swiss claim their famous NUMBERED ACCOUNT was invented as a way to protect Jewish money fleeing Germany

165

from the Nazis' acquisitive eyes. Since the 1930s, however, the accounts have developed into something quite different. As Nicholas Faith puts it in one of the best books on the subject (*Safety in Numbers: The Mysterious World of Swiss Banking*): 'Outside Switzerland, the mere possession of a Swiss bank account, if not actually illegal, is taken as proof of a sophistication bordering on decadence.'

Secured loan. A loan which provides a lender with the right to take over certain prescribed ASSETS of the borrower should the borrower fail to repay. The assets given as SECURITY for the loan may be physical (like property or goods) or they may merely be documents entitling the holder to certain payments.

Banks can sometimes find themselves owning some peculiar things as a result of secured lending that has gone bad. CITICORP has become one of the world's biggest dealers in second-hand aircraft by inheriting planes from INSOLVENT airlines.

Securities. Documents (like share certificates and BONDS) which give the holder the title to the investment. The word is now used loosely to mean the investments themselves.

Some old nineteenth-century bonds on which the borrower DEFAULTED have come to have a new value as works of art, covered as they often are with pretty drawings and foreign writing.

Securities and Exchange Commission (SEC). An American federal agency set up to oversee the SECURITIES industry. The SEC celebrated its fiftieth anniversary in 1984. It has five commissioners and a staff of almost 2,000. There is a tendency for the commissioners to be lawyers, although the current chairman, John Shad, is a former vice-chairman of the big WALL STREET BROKER E. F. Hutton.

The SEC is based in Washington, DC. Its main weapon in the fight to keep the securities markets clean is disclosure: issuers of securities in America have to reveal far more about themselves than securities issuers in any other country. Its current chief preoccupation is the prevention of insider dealing (the use of non-public information to make a profit in securities markets).

Securities Industry Association (SIA). The trade association for over 500 SECURITIES firms based in Canada and the United States. The firms account for about 90 per cent of all the securities business done in North America.

The SIA was set up in 1972 after the merger of two long-established securities associations. It has developed into an extremely powerful lobbying group with a loud voice in Washington's corridors of power. It has consistently opposed any breakdown of the segmentation of COMMERCIAL BANKING and INVESTMENT BANKING created by the GLASS–STEAGALL ACT. Much of its argument has been based on horror stories of what happened in the 1920s, before the Act was in force.

Self-regulatory agency (SRA). A new animal proposed by the GOWER REPORT. SRAs would be formed by different groups (e.g. MERCHANT BANKS, investment advisers, etc.) in the CITY of London to see that their members give adequate protection to investors. Watching over the SRAs could be a rejuvenated COUNCIL FOR THE SECURITIES INDUSTRY; watching over that would be the government.

SRAs would have to be registered with the Department of Trade, which would be the final arbiter of their number. Anyone selling investment services to the public would have to be a member of an SRA or, alternatively, registered directly with the Department.

Settlement day. A day in the life of the London STOCK EXCHANGE. The day at the end of each ACCOUNT when bills for the buying and selling of shares have to be settled. Also called 'pay day'.

Shelf registration. A system introduced in the United States in 1982 to allow companies to file with the SECURITIES AND EXCHANGE COMMISSION (SEC) (in one filing) all the SECURITIES they plan to issue within a two-year period. They can then sell their securities 'off the shelf' as and when they wish and without waiting for the SEC's tiresome filing procedures.

Because shelf registration was authorized by a new ruling from the SEC (Rule 415), off-the-shelf issues are sometimes referred to as Rule 415 issues.

Short-term. A bank loan with an original MATURITY of less than twelve months is a short-term loan. For other than short-term maturities, see MEDIUM-TERM and LONG-TERM.

Sight deposit. Money that can be withdrawn from a bank almost immediately – i.e. CURRENT ACCOUNT deposits, overnight deposits from other banks and money lent AT CALL.

Sight draft. A DRAFT payable on demand, to be distinguished from a USUANCE DRAFT, which is a draft payable at some future date.

Sindona, Michele. A Sicilian financier who became banker to Pope Paul VI and then took on the ultimate challenge – the United States. In the early 1970s he became the biggest shareholder in the FRANKLIN NATIONAL BANK, which then went bust. Mr Sindona went to a New York jail convicted of fraud, misappropriation of bank funds and perjury. In 1984 he was extradicted to face charges in Italy. He is kept busy giving interviews to journalists writing the story of his own spectacular collapse or of that of his lieutenant, ROBERTO CALVI.

Singapore. An Asian island of 2.5 million people (77 per cent of them of Chinese origin) with designs on HONGKONG's mantle as top FINANCIAL CENTRE in the Far East. Singapore is still a not-very-close second, partly because its financial institutions are more tightly controlled than those in Hongkong, partly because there is simply more money in Hongkong.

Singapore hopes to steal a march on Hongkong in the burgeoning business of financial FUTURES. In conjunction with Chicago, it is trying to set up a market to provide round-the-clock dealing. In the end both Singapore and Hongkong could lose out to Australia if the English-speaking antipodean country really set its mind on becoming one of the world's major financial centres.

Single capacity. The separation (particularly strict in Britain) of market-making in SECURITIES from dealing in securities; rather like the distinction between wholesaling and retailing in the rag trade. STOCKBROKERS have the single capacity to be brokers of securities (i.e. agents buying and selling on instructions from investors). Stock JOBBERS have the single capacity to be market-makers (i.e. to hold shares as principals and to set their price). Jobbers cannot be brokers or vice versa. But all that is changing in Britain.

Société Générale. France's third biggest bank, nationalized since 1945. Société Générale was set up in 1864 by a bunch of Parisian businessmen. It has had a strong leaning towards industrial lending ever since.

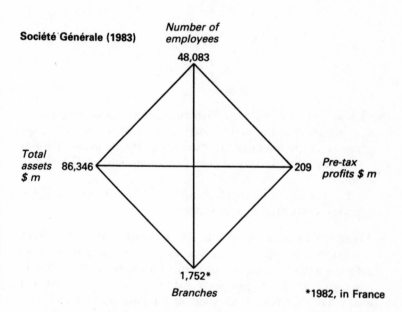

Société Générale (1983)

Number of employees
48,083

Total assets $ m   86,346

209   Pre-tax profits $ m

1,752*
Branches

*1982, in France

Société Générale de Banque. Not to be confused with Société Générale (if that's possible). Société Générale de Banque is Belgium's biggest bank, the child of a merger in 1965 between three banks, two of which had perfectly nice names that would have avoided confusion. The bank specializes in doing EUROPEAN CURRENCY UNIT-denominated business – quite appropriate for the biggest bank in the polyglot Eurocentre of Brussels.

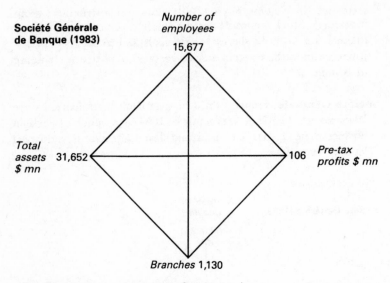

Société Générale de Banque (1983)

Number of employees 15,677

Total assets $ mn 31,652

Pre-tax profits $ mn 106

Branches 1,130

Soft loan. Money lent on soft terms – i.e. terms more generous than those available in the marketplace. Most soft loans are given as aid by national governments or by the INTERNATIONAL DEVELOPMENT ASSOCIATION, the 'soft-loan arm' of the WORLD BANK.

The softness can manifest itself in two forms: as lower INTEREST RATES or as longer MATURITIES.

Solvency. The state of having ASSETS worth more than your LIABILITIES (the opposite of INSOLVENCY). Although supervisors keep a watchful eye on the solvency of banks under their charge, it is usually LIQUIDITY problems that bring about the downfall of banks, not solvency. A shortage of liquidity (i.e. the ability to repay depositors on demand) leads to a RUN on the bank which in turn (if unchecked) leads to insolvency.

Solvency ratio. the ratio between a bank's CAPITAL and its ASSETS (see CAPITAL RATIO).

Solvency is not to be confused with LIQUIDITY. A bank that is not liquid is unable to pay its debts on time; a bank that is insolvent is unable to pay its debts. An illiquid bank can, however, soon become an insolvent bank if it cannot staunch a flood of depositors demanding their money back.

South Sea Bubble. A share whose price gets talked up and up until suddenly people realize that it is little more than hot air. They then sell, everybody else panics, the price falls, and thousands are ruined on the way down.

The original South Sea Bubble was the South Sea Company established in 1710 and given a monopoly on trading in the South Pacific seas. The company because so powerful that it was eventually allowed to buy up the national debt (much smaller then than it is now) before investors lost confidence in the company and the bubble burst.

Sovereign. The British GOLD COIN representing £1 sterling but worth much more. Until 1974 sovereigns were minted only for export to places (like the Middle East) that enjoyed hoarding gold coins. Britons can now buy new ones (as well as half-sovereigns). A sovereign's value reflects the price of gold. It is a standard 7.998 grams (0.25 TROY OUNCES) in weight.

Sovereigns are sometimes called 'kings' and 'queens' to differentiate between the sex of the sovereign whose head is portrayed on the coins.

Spalding Report. A report produced in 1983 by a committee under the chairmanship of Mr John Spalding, chief executive of Britain's biggest BUILDING SOCIETY, the HALIFAX. Its remit was to draw up recommendations on changes in legislation for the societies to present to the government. A lot of fuddy-duddy societies objected to the report's quite reasonable suggestions. So another version (Spalding Mark II) was presented to the government early in 1984. The difference between the first and second versions was scarcely visible.

Special Drawing Right (SDR). The INTERNATIONAL MONETARY FUND's (IMF) own special kind of money. Invented by the IMF in 1967, SDRs first came into operation in 1970 as a sort of RESERVE CURRENCY to supplement national currencies and GOLD as the medium in which countries hold their RESERVES.

The SDR has changed over time. For many years it was an esoteric oddity fully understood only by a few CENTRAL BANKERS. In 1981, however, in an attempt to extend its usage beyond the IMF and its accounts (which are denominated in SDRs), it was simplified. It is now based on a weighted average of only five different currencies: the dollar (with a weight of 42 per cent), the Deutschmark (with a weight of 19 per cent), the French franc, the pound sterling and the yen (each with a weight of 13 per cent).

Since the simplification, usage of the SDR has expanded. Some banks offer deposits and loans denominated in SDRs, and some companies use the SDR as an accounting unit for their trade. Transactions in SDRs monitored by the IMF increased in 1983 to a value of SDR20.7 billion, well up on the previous record year (1982) when the level was SDR12.2 billion.

Specialist. A stockbroker and member of an American STOCK EXCHANGE who acts, in effect, as a stock JOBBER in that he is prepared to make a market in particular shares by buying all those that are offered and selling as and when requested.

Spot price. The buying or selling price quoted for a transaction to be made on the spot, usually referring to transactions in the foreign exchange markets. Spot prices contrast with prices for FUTURES or OPTIONS contracts.

Spread. The difference between the RATE a bank pays for its deposits and the rate it gets for lending them out. The thickness of its spreads is the most significant influence on a bank's profits.

Stag. Someone who hopes to profit from a fixed-price ISSUE of SECURITIES by asking for more securities than he wants. His expectation is that the issue will be oversubscribed. He can then sell his surplus shares at a fat profit as soon as SECONDARY MARKET trading in the issue begins.

Stand-by arrangement. Members of the INTERNATIONAL MONETARY FUND (IMF) have the right to borrow from the Fund a certain percentage of the quota that has been allocated to them. Loans are made available to members under a stand-by arrangement in which the amounts they can borrow, when, for how long, and under what terms, are laid down.

Members have the right to borrow up to 25 per cent of their quotas with no strings attached. When they want to borrow more, they have to agree to meet certain economic conditions known as 'performance criteria'. The more they want to borrow, the tighter these conditions become.

At the end of January 1984 thirty different countries had stand-by arrangements with the IMF. The total amount pledged was SDR14.7 billion, with the biggest amounts going to South Korea (SDR575 million), Chile (SDR500 million), Portugal (SDR445 million) and Hungary (SDR425 million).

Standing order. An instruction from a customer to his bank to make a regular (often monthly) payment of a fixed amount to a named creditor. Useful for making regular payments that do not change too frequently – like those for a MORTGAGE or a life insurance premium.

State-chartered bank. American banks can choose whether to have a charter from their state or from the national authority, the COMPTROLLER OF THE CURRENCY. If they choose to have a state charter, they are regulated by state bank departments. Their interests can be very different from those of the national authorities. Banks have often played one authority off against another to force their way through antiquated geographical restrictions.

State-chartered banks that choose to be members of the federal reserve system are also subject to supervision by the FEDERAL RESERVE BOARD.

Statement. The piece of paper sent out by a bank to its customers at regular intervals detailing the state of their account. Almost invariably, statements reveal unpleasant surprises in their list of debits and credits, bank charges and STANDING ORDERS. In olden times, statements were handwritten by batteries of bank clerks. Now they are churned out at the press of a computer button.

Stock exchange. The physical place ('floor') where SECURITIES are bought and sold; sometimes known by its French name, BOURSE.

Stockbroker. A member of a STOCK EXCHANGE authorized to deal in SECURITIES. A CARTEL – anybody who wants to buy or sell securities has to do so through a stockbroker. For his services the broker charges a COMMISSION. In years when there is a lot of

Table 35   *Stockbrokers*

	Number of quoted company clients	
	end 1983	end 1980
Cazenove	255	254
Rowe & Pitman	143	141
Hoare-Govett	133	130
Grieveson Grant	103	30
Laing & Cruickshank	86	72
de Zoete & Bevan	77	91
L. Messel	69	63
W. Greenwell	62	66
Capel-Cure Myers	62	65
Panmure Gordon	60	61

Source: Crawfords Directory of City Connections.

buying and selling of securities, stockbrokers can make fortunes. In Britain some brokers are reputed to earn more than £1 million in a good year. In the USA, in the bumper year of 1983, many brokers earned more than $1 million.

In different countries different financial institutions are allowed to be stockbrokers. In West Germany and Switzerland the business is dominated by banks. In Britain, because of SINGLE CAPACITY, stockbrokers are nothing but stockbrokers. That is changing. A number of financial institutions have taken stakes of up to 29.9 per cent (the maximum allowed) in British stock-broking firms. Soon they will be allowed to buy more.

Table 36   *Largest British stockbrokers, 1983*
(% market shares of institutional brokerage commissions)

UK equities	%	Gilts	%	Total[1]	%
Hoare-Govett	6	Grieveson Grant	10	Hoare-Govett	7
Wood Mackenzie	5	W. Greenwell	10	Grieveson Grant	6
Scrimgeour Kemp-Gee	5	Mullens	10	James Capel	5
James Capel	5	Hoare-Govett	9	Phillips & Drew	5
Cazenove	5	Phillips & Drew	8	Scrimgeour Kemp-Gee	5
Grieveson Grant	4	L. Messel	6	W. Greenwell	5
Phillips & Drew	4	de Zoete & Bevan	6	Wood Mackenzie	5
de Zoete & Bevan	4	Pembes & Boyle	6	Rowe & Pitman	4
Rowe & Pitman	4	Scrimgeour Kemp-Gee	5	Cazenove	4
L. Messel	3	James Capel	4	de Zoete & Bevan	4

Note:
[1] including foreign equities.   *Source*: City Research Association.

Stop order. An order from an investor to his STOCKBROKER to buy a certain share when it reaches a specified price above the current market price, or to sell when it reaches a named price below the current market price.

Strike price. The price at which PUT OPTIONS and CALL OPTIONS can be exercised. The options are said to be 'in the money' or 'out of the money' depending on whether the difference between the strike price and the price in the SPOT markets is positive or negative.

Sumitomo Bank. In recent years the most successful (i.e. the most profitable) of the twelve big COMMERCIAL BANKS in Japan known as CITY BANKS. Sumitomo owns a bank in California and in 1984 bought the Swiss Banco del Gottardo, one of the few good overseas bits of the ill-fated BANCO AMBROSIANO.

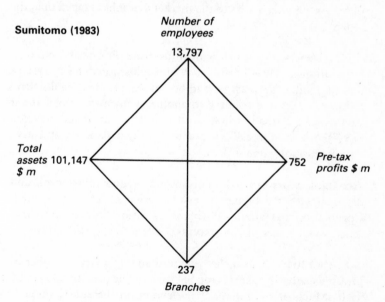

Sumitomo (1983)

Number of employees 13,797

Total assets 101,147 $ m

Pre-tax profits $ m 752

237 Branches

Supplier credit. A loan to an importer (for up to 80 per cent of the purchase price of the goods imported) which is GUARANTEED by the EXPORT CREDIT agency (see EXPORT CREDITS GUARANTEE DEPARTMENT) of the country of the exporter.

Suspense account. A sort of dustbin ACCOUNT (at a bank or elsewhere) into which payments are shunted temporarily while in transit or when there is doubt about their rightful home.

Swap. A transaction in which two parties swap financial ASSETS. In the foreign exchange markets the CENTRAL BANKS of fourteen developed countries have an arrangement whereby if they need to support their currencies, one will swap (for up to one year) some of its own currency for a loan from the other in *its* currency. The first such swap was for $50 million in 1962 between the USA's FEDERAL RESERVE BOARD and the BANQUE DE FRANCE.

The idea of swapping has now spread further. In INTEREST RATE swaps banks arrange for a borrower who has raised, say, Swiss francs to swap them with another borrower who has raised, say, US dollars. This can be to the advantage of both parties. Each may have cheaper access to the market that it has tapped than the other.

SWIFT (Society for Worldwide Inter-bank Financial Telecommunications). SWIFT is a sort of sophisticated telex system owned jointly by a large number of banks. The banks send messages from one country to another with instructions about payments to be made and ACCOUNTS to be credited and debited.

SWIFT started in 1977. It is a non-profit-making co-operative with its headquarters in Brussels.

Swiss Bank Corporation. The second biggest Swiss bank and the one with the biggest overseas network. The Swiss Bank Corporation has about 200 branches inside Switzerland. Like other Swiss banks, it is a UNIVERSAL BANK. See p. 177 above.

Syndicated loan. A loan that is spread among a large number of banks, usually because it is too big for any one bank to take on by itself. Much of the international lending in the EUROMARKET is syndicated. It requires tight (and lengthy) legal documentation to ensure that all lenders agree about what to do should things go wrong with the loan. See Table 37, p. 177 below.

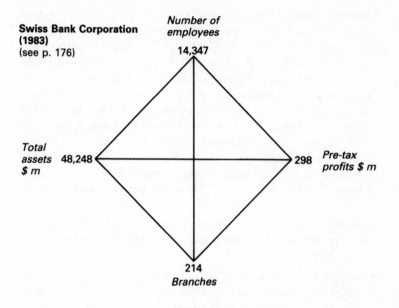

Swiss Bank Corporation (1983)
(see p. 176)

Number of employees 14,347

Total assets $ m 48,248

Pre-tax profits $ m 298

214 Branches

Table 37 *The biggest syndicated Euroloans, 1983*

	Total value $ b
Gulf Oil Corporation	4.28
Petroleos Mexicanos	4.12
Pennzoil	2.50
Kingdom of Sweden	2.45
Kingdom of Denmark	1.73
Republic of Indonesia	1.54
EEC	1.24
Placid Oil Company	1.23
State Energy Commission, W. Australia	1.21
State of California	1.20

Source: Euromoney.

T

Takeover Panel. The short and popular name for the CITY of London's Panel on Takeovers and Mergers. Set up in the 1960s after MERCHANT BANKS were suspected of hanky-panky when advising companies on takeovers, the panel has thirteen members who represent different City interest groups (pension funds, banks, the STOCK EXCHANGE, etc.). It ensures that a set of rules (known as the CITY CODE) are obeyed during takeovers, and it arbitrates in disputes over interpretation of the rules. It has a full-time executive staff (of eleven) housed in the twenty-three-storey stock exchange building.

Since 1983 its chief executive (now Tim Barker) has doubled as the chief executive of the COUNCIL FOR THE SECURITIES INDUSTRY.

Tap stock. A British government BOND ISSUE which is sold by the GOVERNMENT BROKER in dribs and drabs, not all at once.

Telegraphic transfer. A telex or cable sent by a bank to its CORRESPONDENT BANK in another country requesting payment to a named beneficiary in that country. One way of paying for import/export business; the modern form of MAIL TRANSFER.

Ten K. A very detailed report and accounts which QUOTED COMPANIES have to file with the SECURITIES AND EXCHANGE COMMISSION (SEC) in the USA every year. More comprehensive than a company's annual report and accounts for shareholders, it is a fount of information for investigative journalists and takeover speculators. More and more American companies find this (and other disclosure requirements of the SEC) undesirable. Some of them end up being quoted on foreign STOCK EXCHANGES and not on their own.

Tender offer. A method of selling securities developed by the British government and now used all over the world. The seller sets a price (the tender price) at which he is prepared to sell the securities. Offers are invited and applicants state what price they are prepared to pay. (Nothing below the tender price is acceptable.) After a specified time, the securities go to the highest bidders. If enough bids above the tender price have not been received, the offer lapses and the whole ISSUE can be withdrawn.

Term loan. A loan granted for a predetermined length of time (see SHORT-, MEDIUM- and LONG-TERM). A five-year term loan, for example, will be granted for five years, though repayments may be made throughout the period. British banks used to dislike term loans, preferring to give their customers OVERDRAFTS, which could be withdrawn at short notice. They like term loans a bit more now.

Thrifts. General name for those financial institutions in the United States that have the word 'savings' as the first or second word in their title – i.e. SAVINGS AND LOAN ASSOCIATIONS and MUTUAL SAVINGS BANKS.

TIGRS. One of the flowerings of the EUROMARKET's fondness for colourful acronyms. Tigrs is short for Treasury Investment Gross Receipts, an instrument backed by American TREASURY BONDS.

Time deposit. A bank deposit with a specified MATURITY – e.g. three months, six months or one year.

Tombstone. The more tombstones, the less dead is the EURO-MARKET. Tombstones are the advertisements that adorn glossy financial magazines listing banks which have PARTICIPATED in a SYNDICATED LOAN or a BOND ISSUE (see p. 180). The pecking order on the tombstone is all-important. At the top comes the name of the borrower and the amount and terms of the borrowing. Underneath come the banks. The size of the typeface in which their names appear corresponds to their importance in the deal.

The more prestigious the borrower, the keener are the banks to show off on a tombstone. The less prestigious the borrower, the keener is he to show off the names of the banks that are prepared to lend to him (or to UNDERWRITE his bond issue). In the final analysis it is up to the borrower whether a tombstone advertisement appears. He pays for it.

Town clearing. A system for CLEARING CHEQUES between banks within the CITY of London more quickly than through the 'general clearing' – the system for clearing non-City cheques. Cheques for amounts of more than £10,000 are carried round the

U.S. $150,000,000

Texas Instruments International Finance N.V.

11⅞% Guaranteed Notes Due 1991

Payment of principal and interest unconditionally guaranteed by

Texas Instruments Incorporated

MORGAN STANLEY INTERNATIONAL

AMRO INTERNATIONAL Limited	CITICORP CAPITAL MARKETS GROUP
CREDIT SUISSE FIRST BOSTON Limited	DEUTSCHE BANK AKTIENGESELLSCHAFT
FUJI INTERNATIONAL FINANCE Limited	GOLDMAN SACHS INTERNATIONAL CORP.
KLEINWORT, BENSON Limited	MORGAN GRENFELL & CO. Limited
THE NIKKO SECURITIES CO., (EUROPE) S.A	SOCIETE GENERALE DE BANQUE S.A.
SWISS BANK CORPORATION INTERNATIONAL Limited	UNION BANK OF SWITZERLAND (SECURITIES) Limited

ABU DHABI INVESTMENT COMPANY   ALGEMENE BANK NEDERLAND N.V.   AL-MAL GROUP

ARAB BANKING CORPORATION (ABC)   BANCA DEL GOTTARDO   BANKAMERICA INVESTMENT BANKING GROUP

BANK BRUSSEL LAMBERT N.V.   BANK LEU INTERNATIONAL LTD.   BANQUE GENERALE DU LUXEMBOURG S.A.

BANQUE INTERNATIONALE A LUXEMBOURG S.A.   BANQUE NATIONALE DE PARIS

BARCLAYS MERCHANT BANK   BAYERISCHE VEREINSBANK   CAZENOVE & CO.   COMMERZBANK
Aktiengesellschaft   Aktiengesellschaft

COMPAGNIE DE BANQUE ET D'INVESTISSEMENTS, CBI   COPENHAGEN HANDELSBANK A/S   CREDIT LYONNAIS

DAIWA EUROPE   DOMINION SECURITIES AMES   DRESDNER BANK   DREXEL BURNHAM LAMBERT
Limited   Limited   Aktiengesellschaft   Incorporated

EUROMOBILIARE   GIROZENTRALE UND BANK DER ÖSTERREICHISCHEN SPARKASSEN
Aktiengesellschaft

E. F. HUTTON & COMPANY (LONDON)   LLOYDS BANK INTERNATIONAL   LTCB INTERNATIONAL
Limited   Limited   Limited

MANUFACTURERS HANOVER   MITSUBISHI FINANCE INTERNATIONAL
Limited

MITSUBISHI TRUST & BANKING CORPORATION (EUROPE) S.A.   MITSUI FINANCE EUROPE
Limited

THE NATIONAL BANK OF KUWAIT S.A.K.   NIPPON CREDIT INTERNATIONAL (HK) LTD   NOMURA INTERNATIONAL
Limited

NORDDEUTSCHE LANDESBANK   SAL. OPPENHEIM JR. & CIE.   ORION ROYAL BANK
GIROZENTRALE   Limited

PIERSON, HELDRING & PIERSON N.V.   PK CHRISTIANIA BANK (U.K.)   PRUDENTIAL-BACHE
Limited   Securities

N. M. ROTHSCHILD & SONS   SANWA BANK (UNDERWRITERS)   SUMITOMO FINANCE INTERNATIONAL
Limited   Limited

SUMITOMO TRUST INTERNATIONAL   THE TAIYO KOBE BANK (LUXEMBOURG) S.A.
Limited

TOKAI INTERNATIONAL   UNITED OVERSEAS BANK S.A.   VEREINS- UND WESTBANK
Limited   Aktiengesellschaft

YAMAICHI INTERNATIONAL (EUROPE)   YASUDA TRUST EUROPE
Limited   Limited

June 20, 1984

Tombstone advertisement (See p. 179).

City by messengers so that they can be credited to one ACCOUNT and debited from another on the day that they are presented to a bank.

The old-fashioned, messenger-based town clearing system is threatened by the recent arrival of the CLEARING HOUSE AUTO-MATED PAYMENT SYSTEM.

Trade credit. The credit granted by one trader to another. If the trader is exporting, the trade credit becomes an EXPORT CREDIT.

Tranche. The lumps in which a loan is dolloped out if it is not all given to the borrower at once; most frequently used to refer to the dollops in which the INTERNATIONAL MONETARY FUND gives out its loans to member countries. Release of the next tranche of such a loan may be dependent on the borrowers' reaching pre-arranged targets.

Travel and entertainment (T. and E.) cards. Those plastic slivers, like AMERICAN EXPRESS and Diners Club cards, that allow the holder to buy goods (a Porsche, say, or a blue fox fur) up to a higher value than do credit cards. But T. & E. cards give no credit and demand payment immediately on receipt of a monthly statement. Unlike most credit cards, T. & E. cards also charge an annual fee for the privilege of owning one.

The cards rely heavily on creating an image of up-market internationalism about their owners. As more and more people own the cards, the less credible is the image becoming. So the card companies have moved on to providing even more exclusive plastic, like the GOLD CARD. Now even that is dropping from people's 'in' lists, so American Express has invented the platinum card (costing $250 a year) to top them all. What next?

Traveller's cheque. A remarkably clever method of payment invented in the nineteenth century, and since exploited best, by AMERICAN EXPRESS. It is a sort of CASH substitute, acceptable almost anywhere in the world. Its secret is the simple security device of the double signature. That gives the acceptor of the CHEQUE a reasonably sophisticated guarantee that the person signing the cheque in front of him is the person who originally bought it.

The demise of the traveller's cheque has been long predicted in the age of electronic payments. But companies like American Express continue to make huge sums of money from using the cash paid for the cheques (the FLOAT) between the time it is paid in and the time the cheque is used (on average two to three months).

Nobody knows exactly how many traveller's cheques are sold.

The best guesses come from the industry-watcher Spencer Nilson in Los Angeles. He reckons that $41 billion worth were sold in 1983, 48 per cent of that by American Express.

Treasury bill. SHORT-TERM instruments issued by governments, usually repayable in three months. In Britain Treasury BILLS are issued every week (on Friday). For the past four years the weekly amount sold has been £100 million worth. The issue is always fully UNDERWRITTEN by the DISCOUNT HOUSES.

Treasury bills are sold at a DISCOUNT, their YIELD being a leading indicator of the way in which INTEREST RATES are moving.

British banks are big buyers of Treasury bills. They like them because they give brownie points when calculating PRUDENTIAL RATIOS. In the United States Treasury bills are more widely held and there are more of them.

Trigger. Banks rarely give loans with no strings attached. The strings often take the form of conditions to be met by the borrower. If these conditions are not met, then the bank's right to call in the loan (i.e. to get its money back) may be triggered.

Troy ounce. A measure used for weighing GOLD and silver, equal to 1.09714 non-Trojan ounces.

True and fair. A much-loved phrase of accountants: what they try to ensure is achieved in the accounts which they prepare or audit. It is a concept, however, applicable more to the boxing ring than to the accounts of companies. The true and fair view of a company's financial position is rarely, if ever, unique.

Trustee. A person who is entrusted with property belonging to someone else. A trustee can act in many different roles: as the person charged with disposing of a dead man's property according to his will (a job banks often do); as the person charged with looking after the interests of a minor until he or she comes of age; as the person charged with looking after money donated to a charity; or even as the person charged with looking after the editorial integrity and independence of a journal like *The Economist*.

Trustee Savings Bank (TSB). A big British SAVINGS BANK which is set up as four regional, unincorporated societies managed by boards of TRUSTEES. Each of the four societies is a separate bank. They have a central board, set up by statute, which has certain overall supervisory responsibilities for the banks.

The TSB's origins can be traced back to the early nineteenth century and to a small Scottish croft where the savings bank movement, with its focus on the encouragement of thrift, first began (see HENRY DUNCAN).

The TSB movement has changed a lot since then. It has begun to offer a full banking service (including loans to companies) as a step on the way to becoming a conventional PUBLIC COMPANY. It is awaiting an Act of Parliament to be transformed.

Tuke, Anthony. The chairman of BARCLAYS BANK from 1951 to 1962. Known as the Iron Tuke, he is best remembered for his evidence to the RADCLIFFE committee in 1959 in which he said (of Barclays Bank): 'We do not want the public to discuss our affairs. We would much rather they did not. The more information we give them the more they will discuss our affairs, and that is what we do not want.' Many bankers still believe, like sausage-makers, that their business is best conducted in private so as not to upset the consumer. Mr Tuke's son, now Sir Anthony, also became chairman of Barclays Bank.

Turn. The profit made from 'turning over' a particular bit of business. Since most of the bank's business is the taking in of deposits and the making of loans, a bank's turn is the amount of money it earns from charging a higher rate of interest to borrowers than it pays to depositors. The difference between the rates of interest for borrowers and depositors is known as the SPREAD.

U

Underwrite. Agree to buy (alone or as part of a SYNDICATE) the whole of a BOND or share ISSUE. The UNDERWRITER attempts to place the issue with investors who intend to hang on to the security for a while.

If he cannot sell the SECURITIES (if, for example, the pricing of the issue is not right), the underwriter will be left holding the securities himself for longer than he wishes.

Table 38 *The biggest US corporate underwriters, 1983*

	Number of issues	Total value $ b
Salomon Brothers	280	12.72
Merrill Lynch	314	10.85
Goldman, Sachs	238	10.48
First Boston	195	8.39
Drexel Burnham Lambert	146	6.72
Morgan Stanley	125	6.71
Lehman Brothers Kuhn Loeb	134	5.63
Kidder, Peabody	146	3.40
Shearson/American Express	140	2.99
Blyth Eastman Paine Webber	103	2.94

Source: Institutional Investor.

Union Bank of Switzerland. The biggest of the (very) big Swiss banks and a power in the land of the well-scrubbed cow. The bank is a UNIVERSAL BANK with 240 offices throughout Switzerland and more than 17,000 employees.

Switzerland's five biggest banks dominate the country's banking scene, accounting for 50 per cent of the ASSETS of all the banks in Switzerland (including foreign banks). See p. 185 top.

Unit trust. A British form of investment designed to widen share ownership. Unit trusts invest money in shares and other marketable debt on behalf of small investors. The investors hold a unit in the trust; the value of that unit reflects the value of the shares lying behind it. Most British banks have their own stable of unit trusts, which they retail energetically through their branches.

Unit trusts differ from INVESTMENT TRUSTS in that every time

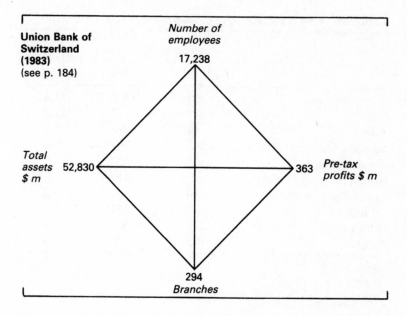

Union Bank of Switzerland (1983) (see p. 184)

Number of employees 17,238

Total assets $ m 52,830

Pre-tax profits $ m 363

294 Branches

more money is put into a unit trust, more 'units' are issued. The only way an investor can buy into an existing investment trust is to buy its existing shares.

The theoretical advantage of a unit trust is that it enables small investors to have a wider PORTFOLIO than if they were investing on their own – and at a much lower cost. In practice, unit trusts have now become very specialized, with some concentrating on a very narrow range of investments (the Papua New Guinea copper mining trust may not be far off). Investors may soon have almost as many unit trusts to choose from as they have individual shares.

In Britain in 1963 there were 1.05 million accounts with seventy-one different unit trusts. By 1983 the number of accounts had almost doubled to 2.04 million, while the number of unit trusts had multiplied almost tenfold (to 630). Gross sales of unit trusts per annum shot up from £77 million in 1963 to £2,460 million in 1983, to give a total of £11,190 million invested in unit trusts. (For the American equivalent, see OPEN-END INVESTMENT FUND.)

Table 39 *Unit trusts: the biggest management groups*

	1982[1]	1983[1]	% share of industry at end 1983
Save & Prosper	1,050	1,335	11.4
M & G	949	1,317	11.3
Allied	644	986	8.4
Barclays Unicorn	592	767	6.6
Henderson	393	728	6.2
Britannia	379	519	4.4
TSB Trust Company	346	500	4.3
Schroder	240	453	3.9
Hill Samuel	271	365	3.1
Target	197	280	2.4

Note:
[1] (£m, 31st December)
Source: Unit Trusts Year Book.

Universal bank. Those banks (commonly found in Switzerland, West Germany and the Netherlands) that are allowed to do almost anything financial, from lending other people's money to UNDERWRITING, advising on investments, stock BROKING, metal broking, etc. Some frown on universal banking in the belief that it creates too many conflicts of interest within one bank. Can a bank give dispassionate advice on a share for which it is underwriter and also broker and banker to the issuer? That question has not stopped foreigners from wanting a Swiss bank ACCOUNT and taking their Swiss banker's investment advice.

German banks own 9 per cent of all West German QUOTED. COMPANIES. Their control of new ISSUES (as STOCK EXCHANGE members) is sometimes blamed for the small number of companies LISTED on German stock exchanges (about 20 per cent of all German LIMITED LIABILITY companies). The banks prefer to lend to good companies rather than to raise new capital for them. And the bad companies? Nobody wants to buy their securities anyway.

Unlisted Securities Market (USM). The London STOCK

EXCHANGE's second tier, set up in November 1980, to enable smaller, less mature companies (those that do not want to go to all the expense and trouble of a full LISTING on the exchange) to get access to the CAPITAL MARKET. The USM is now well-established. More than 230 companies were QUOTED on it at the end of 1983. Their total MARKET CAPITALIZATION was over £2.3 billion.

For VENTURE CAPITAL companies the USM is the pot of gold at the end of the rainbow, the method whereby the companies' founders get their money out of their companies by selling shares to the general public.

Unsecured credit. A loan that has no SECURITY. If a borrower goes bust, the provider of unsecured credit has to wait until all the secured creditors have taken their bite before he has any right to whatever ASSETS are left (if any).

Usuance draft. A DRAFT payable on some specified future date; to be distinguished from a sight draft.

V

Value date. The date on which funds are actually transferred from one bank ACCOUNT to another. This may be specifically pre-arranged with the bank, or it may be determined randomly by, for example, how long it takes to clear a CHEQUE.

Variable rate. An INTEREST RATE that varies in line with some benchmark (like LIBOR). American for FLOATING RATE and the opposite of FIXED RATE.

Venture capital. The money that many believe will prime the pump of the next industrial revolution. Venture capital is money (usually in the form of EQUITY) put up by financial institutions or individuals to back risky industrial and commercial ventures (often high-tech ones) at the beginning of their lives.

Vergleich. West Germany's form of RECEIVERship – a half-way house to BANKRUPTCY. Strict conditions must be met before a company can get into *Vergleich*. Once in, the company can WRITE OFF up to 65 per cent of all its debts before carrying on, almost as before.

First, a company must be unable to pay its bills. Then, if half a company's creditors (representing at least 80 per cent of its debts) agree, a court can approve *Vergleich*. The company's debts are frozen (for eighteen months if it agrees to pay back 35 per cent of its debts, for twenty-four months if it agrees to pay back 40 per cent). The most famous company to go into *Vergleich* in recent years was the electrical giant AEG.

Vergleich is, however, somewhat akin to the eye of a needle for a camel. Less than 1 per cent of troubled companies make it; the rest go straight to the bankruptcy courts. For some the problem lies in persuading creditors to go along with the deal; for others the problem lies in paying their bills (they cannot even afford the court costs associated with *Vergleich*).

Visa. The international co-operative of banks that markets payment systems like TRAVELLER'S CHEQUES and CREDIT CARDS. The most important thing about Visa is its name. When added to the cards or cheques of a bank known in only one country, it makes them recognizable (i.e. acceptable) in any country which has Visa member banks.

There are 202,000 retailers in Britain who accept Visa cards, and 3.7 million around the world in 160 different countries. In 1983 £3,240 million worth of goods were bought in Britain by Visa cardholders; £166 million of that total was accounted for by non-British holders of the cards.

Volcker, Paul. The 6 foot 5-inch, cigar-smoking chairman (since 1979) of America's FEDERAL RESERVE BOARD. Mr Volcker, who has his hands closest to the strings that make American INTEREST RATES twitch, is (arguably) the most powerful man in the world. With that, though, comes the disadvantage of being the American government's whipping boy when interest rates do not drop to the levels the government wants.

Mr Volcker's career has included spells at the London School of Economics, the New York Federal Reserve Bank, CHASE MANHATTAN and the US Treasury.

Vostro account. An expression used by someone at bank A when talking to someone at bank B to refer to the account of bank B with bank A. Based on the Latin *Voster* (*Vester*) meaning 'your' – i.e. 'your account with us'. See NOSTRO ACCOUNT.

W

Waiver. The agreement of a lender to overlook a borrower's failure to meet certain conditions attached to the granting of a loan – conditions which, without a waiver, would give the lender the right to declare the loan in DEFAULT.

Waivers are often granted for a short time on the understanding that the borrower will, by the end of the time, have met the conditions.

Wall Street. More than the 600 yards of prime Manhattan real estate that bears the name: Wall Street is capitalism writ large. Along its length are housed the NEW YORK STOCK EXCHANGE (the world's biggest by far) and the skyscraper offices of the banks and BROKERS who help determine the value of everything from IBM to a dollar bill.

Warburg, S. G. One of Britain's top MERCHANT BANKS and one of its youngest, having been set up in 1934 by the legendary refugee from Nazi Germany, Siegmund Warburg. Mr Warburg, subsequently knighted, died in 1982 at the age of 80.

S. G. Warburg, the bank, won its spurs in the notorious 'Aluminium War' of 1958, when it was banker to Tube Investments in its takeover bid for British Aluminium – a bid that had the serried ranks of the then gentlemanly financial establishment against it. In the end Warburg's side won. The establishment retired in confusion.

Since then Warburg has been one of the few British merchant banks to go international, participating in EUROBOND UNDERWRITING in competition with big continental European banks and the omnipresent Americans, and linking up (less successfully) with the French bank PARIBAS and the American BROKER A. G. Becker.

Warehousing. Disguising the purchase of shares in a company by using NOMINEES and others to buy stakes. These can then act in concert to make a surprise takeover bid for the company or otherwise impose their will. Many countries try to stop this sort of surprise attack by requiring public disclosure of any stake of over 5 per cent held in a company and by laying down rules about the behaviour of CONCERT PARTIES.

Warrant. Two meanings:
- A written instruction that makes legal a payment that would otherwise be illegal.
- The chance given to investors to buy SECURITIES at a prescribed price within a named period.

This second sort of warrant can (like OPTIONS) be bought and sold.

Westpac. Is it a Californian hitchhiker or a new way of wrapping frozen fish? No, it's neither. It is Australia's biggest bank which, for some unknown reason, came up with this extraordinary new name when the Bank of New South Wales and the Commercial Bank of Australia merged in 1981.

Westpac is Australia's third biggest company. It may need all its current brash marketing to fend off competition from FOREIGN BANKS in its domestic market and from ANZ, Australia's second-biggest bank, which in 1984 bought Britain's Grindlays Bank for £182 million.

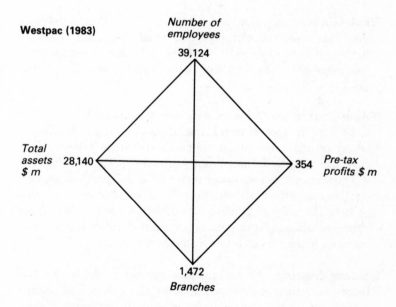

Westpac (1983)

White knight. Somebody who charges out of the blue to rescue a company that is the subject of an unwelcome takeover bid. The white knight puts in a better bid and, supposedly, hangs in there until the undesirable predator skulks away.

Wholesale banking. Banking in big numbers. RETAIL BANKING is the banks' business with their individual customers; wholesale banking is most of the rest – i.e. banking business between banks (see INTER-BANK MARKET) and with other big financial institutions.

Wilson Committee. A bunch of eighteen wise men who were asked in 1977 by the then British Prime Minister, James Callaghan, to report on the value of the country's FINANCIAL SYSTEM. Their chairman was the former Prime Minister, Sir Harold Wilson.

The Committee's 460-page report (plus 307 pages of appendices) was published in 1980. It is still the best written description of how the CITY of London works, but it failed to make any strong recommendations on, in particular, how British industry could be better served by its financial institutions.

Window dressing. What companies (and banks) do, in the days before they finalize their accounts, to make them look as nice as possible. When the majority of companies have the same accounting year (the calendar year in Britain and the United

States; the year to 31 March in Canada and Japan) and they are all busily dressing their windows at the same time, they can have a disturbing effect on financial markets – and on regulators' peace of mind.

Wings. Euro-speak for Warrants into Negotiable Government Securities – a EUROMARKET instrument, with a WARRANT attached, to buy negotiable American government SECURITIES.

Withholding tax. Any tax that is withheld at source – i.e. before the taxpayer has ever seen the INCOME or CAPITAL on which the tax is due. Withholding taxes are most frequently imposed on BOND INTEREST and DIVIDENDS and sometimes on bank interest too. They have great attraction for tax collectors because they make their jobs easier and cut down on the scope for tax evasion.

They also create problems. Double taxation agreements between countries try to ensure that the same income is not taxed twice: first by having tax withheld on it in one country and then by being taxed *post hoc* in another. Those unhappy about such agreements (and determined tax evaders) can almost always take their investments elsewhere, out of the clutches of national tax authorities that impose withholding taxes.

Working capital. What is left over from a company's PAID-UP CAPITAL and RESERVES after all its fixed ASSETS have been bought – i.e. the capital left to work with in running the company's day-to-day business.

World Bank. Common or garden name for the International Bank for Reconstruction and Development, the sister organization of the INTERNATIONAL MONETARY FUND, whose headquarters sit across the road from the World Bank on Washington's H Street. The two are linked by an underground tunnel.

The World Bank was set up in 1944 at the Bretton Woods Conference, itself convened to find a new world monetary order. The bank is now the world's biggest provider of LONG-TERM loans for development in poor countries. To fund its lending it borrows on BOND markets around the world at the very finest RATES. For special sorts of lending the World Bank has two

separate subsidiaries, the INTERNATIONAL DEVELOPMENT ASSOCI-
ATION and the INTERNATIONAL FINANCE CORPORATION.

All the World Bank's presidents have been American:

1946	Eugene Meyer
1947–49	John McCloy
1949–62	Eugene Black
1963–68	George Woods (no relation to Bretton Woods)
1968–81	Robert McNamara
1981–	Alden 'Tom' Clausen

Wriston, Walter. For sixteen years, Mr Big in American COMMER-
CIAL BANKING. Walter Wriston was chairman of the world's
biggest commercial bank (CITICORP) for longer (1968–84) than
any other big-bank chairman. Tough and outspoken, he pulled
no punches in his drive to get American banks permission to do
all the financial things that non-banks could do.

Like many long-serving chiefs, he left the choice of his successor to the last minute. Three men were in the running right to the
end; finally (in June 1984) John Reed got the job.

Writ. A written order from a court commanding someone to do
(or not to do) something.

Write-down. A partial WRITE-OFF. A bank that writes down
(i.e. reduces the value of a loan in its books) does so because it
thinks that it might not be repaid in full. (It will then have less to
write off if the loan proves eventually to be irrecoverable.)

Write-off. What bankers do to debts of which there is no hope of
recovery. When a borrower is, say, BANKRUPT, his bank writes
the loans off its balance sheet by reducing its ASSETS by the value
of the loan. That means the bank has to make an equal and
opposite reduction in the value of its LIABILITIES. This it does by
paring its CAPITAL and RESERVES. A bank that has to write off too
much has, finally, to write itself off.

Y

Yankee bond. A BOND issued in the United States CAPITAL MARKET by a non-American borrower.

Yield. A word used loosely to refer to the annual return on an investment expressed as a percentage. The yield on a bank deposit which pays 8 per cent a year is 8 per cent per annum; the yield from an uncultivated field bought for £30,000 and sold twelve months later for £32,500 is 8.3 per cent ($\frac{2,500}{30,000} \times 100$).

More strictly, the yield is the annual return on a LONG-TERM investment calculated on the assumption that the investment will be held to MATURITY. Take a bond bought for £75 which matures in five years' time. On maturity it is cashed in for £100. Say the COUPON on the bond is 8 per cent. The yield will be more than 8 per cent and will take into account the DISCOUNTED CASH FLOW value of the £25 capital gain to be made over the five years.